Hecate:: The Triple Goddess Revealed

Victoria Collins

Published by Victoria Collins, 2023.

HECATE:: THE TRIPLE GODDESS REVEALED

First edition. August 25, 2023.

Copyright © 2023 Victoria Collins.

ISBN: 979-8223352839

Written by Victoria Collins.

Chapter 1: Introduction.

In this book, we embark on a journey to explore the truly magical and mystical figure of Hecate and discover her rich mythology. Hecate, a goddess of ancient Greek origin, holds a prominent place in the pantheon, with a multifaceted and enigmatic presence that has fascinated scholars and enthusiasts alike. In this introductory section, we will provide an overview of Hecate's origins, her mythological context, and her significant role within Greek mythology.

Hecate's origins can be traced back to ancient Greek religion, where she emerged as a revered goddess with a complex set of attributes and associations. While the exact origins of her worship remain a subject of scholarly debate, her prominence increased during the Hellenistic and Roman periods, when she became a key figure in mystical traditions and magical practices.

Within Greek mythology, Hecate occupies a unique position. She embodies the liminal spaces and transitions, serving as a guide, guardian, and mediator. Hecate's realm of influence encompasses crossroads, boundaries, magic, the moon, witchcraft, and the spirit world. Her role as a goddess of the Underworld further adds to her mystique, as she acts as a psychopomp, guiding souls on their journey between the realms of the living and the dead.

As we explore Hecate's mythological context, we encounter her connections to other deities and prominent myths. Her association with the goddess Persephone, particularly in the context of the abduction myth, underscores her role as a companion and guide within the realm of the dead. Additionally, Hecate's involvement in the journey of the hero Orpheus to the Underworld highlights her power as a facilitator of otherworldly quests and her ability to navigate the depths of the realm of Hades.

Understanding the significance of Hecate in Greek mythology is crucial to appreciating her enduring appeal. Hecate's multifaceted nature reflects the complexities of human existence, encapsulating both light and darkness, transitions and thresholds, and the interplay between the mortal and divine realms. Her association with witchcraft and magic further underscores her role as a protector and facilitator of mystical knowledge, providing a gateway to deeper insights and hidden realms.

In this book, we will delve into Hecate's mythology, symbolism, rituals, and cultural impact. We will explore her various roles, including her connection to the Underworld as a guide of souls, her association with witchcraft and magic, and her significance in the lives of ancient Greeks and beyond. By unravelling the layers of Hecate's mythology and delving into her intricate web of symbolism and influence, we will gain a deeper understanding of this captivating goddess and the timeless wisdom she embodies.

Historical Development:

Hecate's worship and significance evolved over time, reflecting the cultural shifts and influences that shaped ancient Greek religion. While her exact origins remain unclear, Hecate's prominence increased during the Hellenistic and Roman periods, particularly in magical and mystical traditions.

Hecate's association with witchcraft, magic, and the unseen realms became more pronounced during this time. She was often invoked for her protective powers, particularly in matters related to childbirth, women's health, and the home. Hecate's connection to crossroads, boundaries, and transitions also expanded, with her role as a guide and guardian gaining prominence.

Worship of Hecate:

The worship of Hecate was diverse and widespread throughout ancient Greece and extended into the Hellenistic and Roman eras. Her worship took various forms, ranging from public ceremonies to private rituals performed by individuals or families. Here are some notable aspects of Hecate's worship:

Public Festivals:

Hecate was honoured in public festivals, including the Grand Rite of the Deipnon, which took place on the last day of the lunar month. These festivals involved processions, offerings, and rituals performed at crossroads or sacred sites associated with Hecate.

Private Rituals:

Individuals and households paid homage to Hecate through personal rituals and offerings. Small altars or shrines dedicated to Hecate were often found in homes, where devotees would leave offerings such as food, herbs, or small statues as a sign of respect and to seek her protection.

Magical Practices:

Hecate played a significant role in magical and mystical traditions. Practitioners of magic sought her assistance in spells, divination, and communication with the spirit world. Magical rituals dedicated to Hecate often involved the use of herbs, incantations, and special symbols to invoke her powers.

Temples and Sanctuaries:

Hecate had dedicated temples and sanctuaries in various parts of Greece. Notably, her temple at Lagina in Caria (now modern-day Turkey) was renowned and served as a centre for her worship. These sacred spaces provided devotees with opportunities for prayer, offerings, and ceremonies.

Associations with Mystery Cults:

Hecate's connections to the Underworld and her role as a guide of souls aligned her with mystery cults, which were secretive religious organisations focused on initiation and the pursuit of spiritual enlightenment. Hecate's mysteries were likely practiced in certain regions, although details of these cults remain elusive.

It is important to note that Hecate's worship was not limited to Greece alone. Her veneration extended to regions influenced by Greek culture, including parts of Anatolia and Italy. The spread of the Hellenistic and Roman Empires further contributed to the diffusion of Hecate's worship and her incorporation into syncretic religious practices.

Chapter 2: The Mythological Persona of Hecate

Genealogy:

Hecate's genealogy and relation to other deities in Greek mythology can be traced through various sources, although there are some variations and interpretations. Here is an overview of Hecate's genealogy and her connections to other important figures:

The myth surrounding Hecate's birth varies in different versions of Greek mythology. One of the most commonly mentioned accounts is found in Hesiod's Theogony. According to this myth, Hecate is the daughter of the Titans Perses and Asteria.

In the myth, Perses and Asteria were siblings, and Asteria had caught the eye of the powerful Titan Zeus. However, Asteria, not wanting to be pursued by Zeus, transformed herself into a quail and flew into the sea. From this union with the sea, she gave birth to Hecate.

Hecate's birthplace is often associated with the island of Delos, although other versions of the myth mention other locations. After her birth, Hecate was taken to Olympus, where she was nurtured by the goddesses Artemis and Selene. This connection to the lunar goddess Selene further reinforces Hecate's association with the moon and her role as a goddess of the night.

It is important to note that Greek mythology consists of various interpretations and versions of stories, and the details of Hecate's birth may differ depending on the source. Nonetheless, the myth of Hecate's birth highlights her divine lineage and her connection to powerful celestial forces, which played a significant role in shaping her characteristics and her subsequent importance in Greek mythology.

Hecate is often depicted as a sister to two prominent Titans, namely Leto and Astraeus. Leto is the mother of the twin gods Apollo and Artemis, while Astraeus is associated with the winds and stars. This sibling connection places Hecate in the celestial and divine sphere, further emphasising her association with the night and the luminous heavens.

In some versions, Hecate is said to be a daughter of Zeus, the king of the gods, and the Titaness Asteria. This lineage further strengthens her divine status and association with the Olympian pantheon.

Hecate shares a close relationship with Persephone, the daughter of Demeter and Zeus, who becomes the Queen of the Underworld after her abduction by Hades. Hecate acts as a companion and guide to Persephone during her time in the Underworld. Their connection reinforces Hecate's role as a deity associated with the realm of the dead and the transitions between life and death.

Hecate is often associated with the goddess Artemis, who is also linked to the moon and the wilderness. Some sources suggest that Hecate served as a nursemaid or mentor to Artemis, guiding her in the ways of the hunt and moon magic. This association further emphasises Hecate's connection to the natural world, magic, and feminine power.

In Greek mythology, Hecate is not typically associated with romantic love or portrayed as having romantic relationships like some other goddesses. Her focus and associations are more centred around magic, witchcraft, the night, the moon, and the underworld. However, there are a few instances where Hecate is mentioned in relation to other gods or figures:

In one account, Hecate is said to have been in love with the sun god Helios. However, Helios did not reciprocate her feelings, which resulted in Hecate feeling rejected and becoming jealous. This unrequited love is sometimes mentioned in myths but is not a central aspect of Hecate's character or mythology.

Hecate is also associated with the god Hermes, who is known as a messenger of the gods and a guide to the underworld. They are sometimes depicted as working together or having a close relationship due to their shared roles in guiding souls and traversing between realms.

It's important to note that Hecate's mythology and associations are primarily focused on her roles as a guardian, guide, and mistress of magic, rather than romantic relationships. Her significance lies more in her powers and attributes related to witchcraft, crossroads, liminal spaces, and the underworld. These aspects make her a fascinating and powerful figure in Greek mythology, but her loves and romantic connections are not as prominent as in the stories of other gods and goddesses.

Hecate's genealogy and relationships with other deities showcase her connections to celestial forces, the Underworld, and other significant figures in Greek mythology. These connections further amplify her status as a powerful and influential goddess associated with magic, transitions, and the mysteries of the cosmos.

Key myths and stories associated with Hecate:

Hecate and Persephone:

The myth of Persephone's abduction by Hades is a well-known story in Greek mythology. It explains the origins of the changing seasons and the ancient Greek belief in the existence of the underworld. Here's a detailed account of the myth:

Persephone, the daughter of the harvest goddess Demeter and the king of the gods, Zeus, was a radiant and beautiful young maiden. She spent her days joyfully wandering through fields, picking flowers, and revelling in the bountiful beauty of nature.

One day, as Persephone was frolicking in a meadow, the earth beneath her split open, and Hades, the god of the underworld, emerged from the depths in his chariot. Hades, struck by Persephone's beauty, became infatuated with her, and resolved to make her his queen and the goddess of the underworld.

In a swift and audacious move, Hades grabbed Persephone and abducted her, taking her down into the dark depths of the underworld against her will. Persephone's cries for help went unanswered as she was whisked away to the realm of the dead.

Meanwhile, Demeter, consumed by grief and despair upon discovering her daughter's disappearance, embarked on an arduous search. She wandered the earth, grieving and mourning the loss of Persephone. During this time, Demeter neglected her duties as the goddess of the harvest, and the land suffered. Crops withered, plants wilted, and famine loomed over the mortal realm.

It is Hecate who hears Demeter's cries and comes to her aid. Hecate guides Demeter to the sun god Helios, who reveals the truth about Persephone's whereabouts. Together, Hecate and Demeter approach

Zeus, seeking his intervention to secure Persephone's release from the underworld.

Zeus, instructed Hermes, the messenger god, to negotiate with Hades. They struck a compromise: Persephone would spend six months of the year with Hades in the underworld as his queen, and the remaining six months, she would be allowed to return to the surface to be reunited with her mother.

Thus, the myth explains the cycle of the seasons. When Persephone is with her mother Demeter on Earth, Demeter's joy at her daughter's return brings about the blooming of flowers and the abundance of the harvest, leading to spring and summer. But when Persephone returns to the underworld, Demeter mourns, causing the land to become barren and winter to descend.

The story of Persephone's abduction serves as a metaphorical explanation for the natural cycle of life, death, and rebirth that occurs in the changing seasons. It also portrays the grief and longing of a mother separated from her daughter and the transformative power of love and compromise.

The myth of Persephone's abduction has been a subject of inspiration for countless artists, writers, and poets throughout history, and it continues to captivate and resonate with audiences today.

Hecate and the Heroines of Troy:

In the epic poem "The Metamorphoses" by Ovid, Hecate appears during the Trojan War as a divine presence aiding the Greek heroines who have been captured by the Trojans.

The myth of Hecate and the Heroines of Troy is a lesser-known tale that highlights Hecate's connection to magic, crossroads, and the realm of the dead. This myth takes place after the fall of Troy and explores the fate of the Trojan women, who are often referred to as the Heroines of Troy.

According to the myth, after the Greek victory in the Trojan War, the surviving Trojan women were captured and enslaved by the victorious Greeks. These women, who had once been noble and respected in their homeland, now found themselves in a state of despair and loss. They were separated from their families, homes, and the lives they once knew.

Feeling the anguish and suffering of the Heroines of Troy, Hecate, as the goddess associated with magic and the underworld, took pity on these women. She heard their cries and saw their struggle to find meaning and hope in their new reality. Moved by their plight, Hecate decided to intervene and offer them solace.

Hecate appeared before the Heroines of Troy, presenting herself as a wise and compassionate guide. She offered them a way to navigate the challenges they faced and find a path towards healing and empowerment. Drawing upon her magical abilities, Hecate guided the Heroines through a series of transformative rituals and initiations.

At the heart of these rituals was the power of the crossroads, symbolising the intersection of choices and possibilities. Hecate led the Heroines to a sacred crossroads, where they were encouraged to reflect upon their past and embrace the potential for a new beginning. It was here that Hecate bestowed upon them her wisdom and teachings, helping them tap into their inner strength and resilience.

Through their interactions with Hecate, the Heroines of Troy discovered their own latent powers and abilities. Hecate taught them the secrets of magic, empowering them to channel their grief and sorrow into acts of personal transformation. They learned to harness their emotions, to embrace their pain as a source of strength, and to navigate the liminal spaces of their lives with confidence and grace.

Under Hecate's guidance, the Heroines of Troy became symbols of resilience and empowerment. They used their newfound knowledge and magical skills to reclaim their sense of agency and forge their own paths in a world that had been shattered. In this way, Hecate's intervention transformed the Heroines from captives to heroines, from victims to powerful agents of change.

Hecate and the Heroines of Aeneas:

In Virgil's epic poem "The Aeneid," Hecate appears as a powerful goddess who aids the hero Aeneas and his companions during their perilous journey. She provides them with protective charms and guides them through the treacherous underworld, ensuring their safe passage. This myth highlights Hecate's association with magic, her role as a guide in the realm of the dead, and her assistance to those on important quests.

Hecate and Circe:

The myth of Hecate and Circe involves two powerful and enchanting figures from Greek mythology. Here's a detailed account of their connection:

Hecate, the goddess of witchcraft, magic, and the night, was known for her knowledge of herbs, potions, and spells. Circe, on the other hand, was a powerful sorceress and enchantress, skilled in the arts of transformation and magic. Both Hecate and Circe held sway over the mystical and supernatural realms, making them kindred spirits in many ways.

According to some versions of the myth, Hecate took Circe under her wing as a mentor and teacher, guiding her in the intricacies of magic and witchcraft. Hecate imparted her vast knowledge and secrets to Circe, allowing her to develop her own formidable powers.

Circe, in turn, became renowned for her ability to transform humans into animals and for her talent in brewing powerful potions. She often used her magic to manipulate and control others, including the men who arrived on her island. However, despite her formidable skills, Circe recognised the wisdom and influence of Hecate and held great respect for her.

Their association also extended to the realm of the night and the moon. Both Hecate and Circe had connections to lunar phases and were often associated with the powers and mysteries of the night. Hecate was often depicted as carrying torches to illuminate the path, while Circe was known to perform her magical rituals and incantations under the light of the moon.

The myth of Hecate and Circe serves as a testament to the influence and knowledge of these powerful female figures in Greek mythology. It highlights their shared mastery of magic, their affinity for the mystical realms, and their ability to shape and manipulate the world around them.

While their individual stories often take centre stage, their connection serves as a reminder of the interwoven nature of the divine and the magical in Greek mythology. Together, Hecate and Circe exemplify the potent and transformative powers of witchcraft, showcasing the importance of female empowerment and the central role of women in the mythological landscape.

These key myths and stories offer glimpses into Hecate's various roles and associations within Greek mythology. They showcase her involvement in the journeys of other deities, her role as a guide and protector, and her association with magic and witchcraft. Through these narratives, Hecate emerges as a complex and influential goddess, weaving her presence into the fabric of ancient Greek mythology and enriching the tapestry of divine tales.

Jason and the Golden Fleece:

In the myth of Jason's quest for the Golden Fleece, Hecate plays a significant role in assisting Jason and his crew. The story goes that Jason, accompanied by his band of heroes known as the Argonauts, embarked on a perilous journey to retrieve the Golden Fleece, a symbol of kingship and prosperity.

As they sailed through treacherous waters and encountered numerous challenges, Hecate aided Jason on multiple occasions. One of the notable instances is when the Argonauts found themselves stranded in a swampy and perilous region known as the Strophades Islands. The islands were infested with deadly birds known as the Harpies, who tormented the crew and prevented their progress.

In their desperate situation, Hecate appeared to Jason in a vision and instructed him to construct a massive bronze clapper. With this clapper, known as the "clangorous brazen thing," Jason was able to scare away the Harpies and free his crew from their torment. Hecate's guidance and intervention proved crucial in overcoming this obstacle and progressing on their quest.

Additionally, it is believed that Hecate provided Jason with magical herbs and potions to protect and strengthen the Argonauts during their perilous journey. She was revered as a goddess of magic and enchantments, and her assistance was sought by heroes in their quests and endeavours.

While Hecate's direct involvement in the quest for the Golden Fleece may not be as prominent as other characters like Medea or Hera, her aid and guidance demonstrate her role as a supernatural ally to those who sought her favour. Her association with magic and her ability to provide assistance in times of need further solidify her status as a powerful and influential deity in Greek mythology.

Chapter 3: Symbols, attributes, and iconography of Hecate

This chapter explores the symbols, attributes, and iconography associated with Hecate.

Torch:

One of the most prominent symbols of Hecate is the torch. She is often depicted holding two torches, which represent her role as a guiding light in the darkness. The torches symbolise her ability to illuminate the path, both in the physical and metaphorical sense, and guide souls through transitions and liminal spaces.

The torch that Hecate is often depicted carrying represents illumination and guidance. As the goddess of the night and the underworld, Hecate possesses the ability to navigate and traverse the darkness. The torch acts as a literal and metaphorical light in the darkness, allowing her to see and guide others through the hidden paths and liminal spaces.

The torch also symbolises Hecate's knowledge and wisdom. With her extensive understanding of magic, witchcraft, and the mysteries of the night, Hecate possesses deep insights into the hidden realms and the unseen forces of the world. The torch represents the illumination of this esoteric knowledge, which she uses to guide and empower those who seek her assistance.

The torch is also associated with Hecate's protective role. As a guardian of crossroads, Hecate ensures the safety of travellers and those at crossroads, both literal and metaphorical. The torch serves as a beacon of light that wards off potential dangers and offers a sense of security to those under her watchful care.

In some interpretations, the torch represents the transformative aspect of Hecate's power. It symbolises the fire of change and initiation, as Hecate is often associated with transitions, rites of passage, and the transformative forces of magic. The torch can be seen as the catalyst that ignites the process of personal growth, allowing individuals to embrace their own power and embark on new journeys.

Keys:

The symbolic keys that Hecate is often portrayed holding in Greek mythology carry various meanings and interpretations. The keys held by Hecate represent her role as a guardian and holder of the keys to the mysteries. As a goddess associated with witchcraft, magic, and the underworld, Hecate possesses knowledge of the hidden realms and esoteric wisdom. The keys symbolise her authority to grant access to these mysteries, granting individuals the opportunity to explore the depths of their own psyche and the hidden realms of existence.

The keys also represent Hecate's association with transitions and passages. As the goddess of crossroads, Hecate presides over liminal spaces where choices are made and paths diverge. The keys signify her ability to unlock the gateways between realms, facilitating the movement and transition between different states of being.

The keys held by Hecate also symbolise her authority and power. They represent her control over the realms she governs, including the underworld and the magical realms. The keys are a tangible representation of her ability to unlock and access these domains, underscoring her position as a formidable and influential deity.

In some interpretations, the keys are seen as protective symbols. They represent Hecate's role as a guardian and protector, ensuring the safety and well-being of those under her care. The keys serve as metaphoric keys to safety, warding off harm and providing a sense of security to those who seek her assistance.

Finally, Hecate's keys illustrate her ability to unlock the mysteries of the unseen realms, guide individuals through transitions, and provide protection and security. The keys serve as potent symbols of Hecate's influence and the transformative potential that lies within her realm of magic and witchcraft.

Crossroads:

Hecate's association with crossroads in Greek mythology is significant and multi-faceted. Crossroads are considered liminal spaces, where two or more paths intersect. They symbolise the meeting point between different realms, such as the physical and the spiritual, the known and the unknown. Hecate is often depicted as a liminal goddess, capable of traversing and overseeing these boundary spaces, making her an appropriate deity to preside over crossroads.

Crossroads represent moments of decision-making and choice. They embody the concept of making a pivotal decision that can alter one's path or destiny. Hecate, as the goddess of transitions and choices, is often invoked at crossroads to seek her guidance in making important life decisions or embarking on new paths. She is believed to possess the ability to illuminate the different options and offer insight into the potential outcomes.

Hecate is regarded as a guardian and protector at crossroads. It was believed that she could ward off evil spirits and provide protection to those who invoked her at these significant intersections. In this role, Hecate is seen as a powerful deity who offers guidance and safeguards those who find themselves at crossroads, both physically and metaphorically.

Crossroads hold a mystical quality and are often associated with magic and witchcraft. They were considered places where magic rituals and offerings could be performed. Hecate, as a goddess associated with magic and witchcraft, was believed to grant her devotees access to hidden knowledge and supernatural powers when invoked at crossroads.

Crossroads were sometimes seen as entrances to the realm of the dead or the Underworld. Hecate, being a goddess associated with the Underworld, held the keys to these realms and was believed to have the ability to guide souls between the worlds. Her association with crossroads reinforces her role as a psychopomp, guiding souls on their journey after death.

Serpents and Dogs:

Hecate's association with serpents and dogs in Greek mythology is intriguing and adds depth to her symbolism. She is often depicted accompanied by serpents, which may be coiled around her arms or entwined in her hair. Serpents have been revered throughout various cultures as symbols of transformation, wisdom, and healing. In Hecate's context, serpents can represent her connection to the mysteries of the earth, the shedding of old patterns, and the transformative power of her magic. Serpents are also associated with the chthonic realm, reinforcing Hecate's ties to the Underworld.

Dogs are another common symbol associated with Hecate. They are often depicted as her loyal companions, either by her side or at her feet. Dogs have a long-standing connection to the spiritual realm and the supernatural. In Greek mythology, they are known as guardians and guides, possessing acute senses and the ability to see what is hidden. Dogs also have a strong association with the Underworld, where they are believed to accompany Hecate as she traverses its realms.

Black dogs in particular, are associated with Hecate. They are seen as her sacred animals and are believed to be her familiars or messengers. They represent her connection to the night, darkness, and the unseen realms. Black dogs are symbolic of her protective and watchful nature, guarding the crossroads and guiding those who seek her guidance.

The serpents symbolise transformation and the chthonic forces, while the dogs embody protection, guidance, and her link to the Underworld. Together, these symbols enhance the mystique and power associated with Hecate, portraying her as a formidable goddess with deep connections to both the earthly and the divine realms.

Lunar Symbolism:

Hecate's association with the Moon and its various phases is significant in Greek mythology and adds to her mystical and transformative qualities. Here are more details about why Hecate is closely linked to the Moon:

Hecate is often referred to as the Triple Goddess, representing the three phases of the Moon: the waxing Moon, the full Moon, and the waning Moon. This association with the lunar cycle highlights her connection to the rhythms of nature, the cycles of life, and the mysteries of transformation. As a Triple Goddess, she embodies the maiden, mother, and crone aspects, each corresponding to a specific phase of the Moon.

The Moon has long been associated with feminine energy, intuition, and the ebb and flow of emotions. It represents the divine feminine, intuition, and the subconscious. Hecate's association with the Moon reflects her embodiment of these qualities. She is seen as a goddess of feminine power, wisdom, and intuition, guiding individuals through the shadows of the night and the depths of the subconscious.

Hecate's connection to the Moon is also tied to her role as a goddess of the night and darkness. The Moon, as it shines in the night sky, provides illumination in the darkness, just as Hecate's torches guide travellers in the night. This association with the Moon emphasises her ability to navigate the unseen and mysterious realms, including the Underworld, and to offer guidance and protection in times of darkness or uncertainty.

The Moon's cycles have long been used as a guide for magical practices and divination. Hecate, as a goddess associated with magic and witchcraft, draws upon the energies of the Moon to enhance her powers. The different phases of the Moon are believed to influence different aspects of magic, and invoking Hecate during specific lunar phases can amplify spell work, rituals, and divination practices.

Throughout history, various lunar festivals and rituals have been dedicated to Hecate. These celebrations often coincide with specific phases of the Moon, such as the new Moon or the full Moon. Devotees of Hecate may perform rituals, offerings, or meditations during these times to connect with her lunar energy and seek her guidance and blessings.

In summary, Hecate's close association with the Moon stems from her embodiment of the Triple Goddess, her connection to feminine energy and intuition, her role as a goddess of the night and darkness, her ties to magic and divination, and the observance of lunar festivals and rituals dedicated to her. The Moon serves as a powerful symbol of transformation, intuition, and the mysteries of the night, all of which are reflected in Hecate's multifaceted nature. We will explore her associations with the moon in more detail in Chapter 4.

Triple Form:

Hecate is sometimes depicted in her triple form, known as the triplicate goddess. This representation shows her as a three-headed or three-bodied deity, symbolising her dominion over the three realms: the heavens, the earth, and the underworld. It also represents her triple nature as a maiden, mother, and crone, reflecting the stages of a woman's life.

These include:

Maiden - The maiden aspect represents the youthful, innocent, and independent stage of a woman's life. In Hecate's triple form, she embodies the maiden archetype, symbolising new beginnings, potential, and the energy of youth. The maiden aspect of Hecate is associated with growth, exploration, and the awakening of feminine power. She is often depicted as a young woman, full of vitality and curiosity.

Mother – The mother aspect represents fertility, nurturing, and creation. Hecate's mother aspect represents the nurturing and protective qualities of the divine feminine. As the mother archetype, she is associated with fertility, childbirth, and the nurturing of life. Hecate's mother aspect embodies compassion, caretaking, and the powerful bond between mother and child. She is often depicted as a mature woman, exuding wisdom, and maternal strength.

Crone - The crone aspect represents wisdom, transformation, and the culmination of life experiences. Hecate's crone aspect symbolises the wisdom gained through the passage of time, the mysteries of death and rebirth, and the transformative power of aging. The crone archetype is associated with intuition, magic, and deep spiritual insight. Hecate's crone aspect embodies wisdom, inner strength, and the ability to traverse the realms of the conscious and the unconscious. She is often depicted as an older woman, sometimes with a veil or cloak, representing her connection to the mysteries of life and death.

The Triplicate Goddess represents the cyclical nature of life, with the maiden embodying beginnings, the mother representing growth and nurturing, and the crone embodying wisdom and transformation. Together, these aspects of Hecate encompass the full spectrum of feminine energy and offer guidance and inspiration to individuals seeking empowerment, personal growth, and a deeper connection to the divine feminine.

Wands and Staffs:

Hecate is occasionally depicted holding a wand or staff that is often entwined with serpents. This depiction holds significant symbolism and adds to Hecate's mystical and transformative qualities. Here are more details about the symbolism of Hecate's wand or staff entwined with serpents:

The wand or staff is a symbol of authority and power, often associated with magic and the ability to command or manipulate energies. As a goddess of magic and witchcraft, Hecate wields this wand or staff as a symbol of her magical authority and influence. It represents her ability to channel and direct supernatural forces, bridging the realms of mortal and divine. It is thought amongst many, that she would use this staff to draw protection circles as part of spell work, the first known account of this practice.

The serpents entwined around Hecate's wand or staff carry their own symbolic meaning. Serpents are often associated with wisdom, regeneration, and transformation. In Greek mythology, serpents were also associated with the chthonic realm, the underworld, and the mysteries of the Earth. The serpents entwined with Hecate's wand or staff signify her connection to these realms and her power over transformative energies.

Serpents have long been associated with healing and rebirth due to their ability to shed their skin and emerge renewed. Hecate's wand or staff, entwined with serpents, help symbolise her role as a healer and guide through transformative experiences. It represents her ability to assist individuals in navigating their personal journeys of healing, growth, and spiritual transformation.

The serpent, often depicted as a wise creature in mythology, is a symbol of wisdom and hidden knowledge. Hecate, as a goddess associated with wisdom and the mysteries of the night, carries the serpents as a symbol of her deep understanding and connection to esoteric knowledge. The entwined serpents on her wand or staff signify her role as a keeper of hidden wisdom and her ability to reveal profound insights to those who seek her guidance.

The combination of the wand or staff with entwined serpents in Hecate's depictions underscores her authority in the realm of magic, her connection to transformative energies, her role as a healer and guide, and her association with hidden wisdom.

Offerings, rituals, and festivals dedicated to Hecate.

Hecate played a significant role in religious practices and cults in ancient Greece. Her worship and cultic practices varied across different regions and time periods, but there were certain elements that were commonly associated with her cult. Here are some aspects of Hecate's role in religious practices and cults:

Personal Devotion:

Hecate was revered as a powerful goddess associated with various aspects of life, including magic, witchcraft, crossroads, and protection. Many individuals and households sought her blessings and guidance in their daily lives. By setting up personal altars or shrines, they expressed their devotion and established a direct connection with Hecate.

The setup of an altar or shrine dedicated to Hecate would typically involve a designated space within the home or outdoors where offerings, symbols, and representations of Hecate could be placed. The altar could be as simple or elaborate as the devotee desired, depending on their resources and personal preferences.

Offerings played a significant role in personal devotion to Hecate. Devotees would present offerings to honour and appease the goddess, seeking her favour and protection. Common offerings included food and drink such as honey, eggs, garlic, bread, or pomegranates. These offerings symbolised sustenance, abundance, and fertility. Candles or lamps were also commonly used to represent the element of fire and to illuminate the sacred space.

Individuals would often place symbols and representations of Hecate on their altars or shrines. These could include statues or figurines depicting Hecate in her various forms, such as the triple goddess or with her associated animals like dogs or serpents. Images or artwork representing her symbols, such as torches, keys, or crescent moons, could also be included. These objects served as focal points for devotion and reminders of Hecate's presence and influence.

Devotees would engage in rituals and prayers at their personal altars or shrines. These practices could involve lighting candles or lamps, offering prayers of gratitude, seeking guidance, or asking for protection. Some individuals might also engage in divination or spell work, calling upon Hecate's assistance in matters of magic or seeking her insights into the unseen realms.

Public Festivals:

Hecate was honoured in various public festivals and ceremonies in ancient Greece, often held at crossroads or sacred sites associated with her.

Hecate had several festivals dedicated to her throughout the year, with the most significant being the Deipnon, which occurred on the last day of the lunar month. During these festivals, communities would come together to honour and appease Hecate. Processions would be held, with participants carrying torches or lamps to symbolise Hecate's role as a goddess of light and guidance.

Crossroads held great significance in Hecate's worship. These liminal spaces were seen as points of transition and connection between different realms. Public ceremonies honouring Hecate would often take place at crossroads, where altars or shrines dedicated to her would be set up. Participants would gather at these crossroads, offer prayers and offerings to Hecate, and perform rituals to seek her protection, guidance, and blessings.

Public ceremonies dedicated to Hecate involved the offering of sacrifices to the goddess. These sacrifices typically included animals such as dogs, honey, eggs, or other symbolic items. The goal was to honour Hecate and establish a reciprocal relationship with her, seeking her favour and protection for the community.

Public ceremonies honouring Hecate often involved ritual performances. These performances could include dramatic presentations, music, dancing, or recitations of hymns and poetry dedicated to the goddess. They served to evoke the presence of Hecate and express reverence for her through artistic and ritualistic means.

Magic and Witchcraft:

Hecate was closely associated with magic and witchcraft in ancient Greece, and she was considered the patroness of practitioners of the mystical arts.

Hecate was often invoked by those practicing sorcery and witchcraft as she was believed to possess extensive knowledge of spells, potions, and enchantments, making her a powerful ally for witches and sorcerers seeking her aid in their magical endeavours. Hecate's association with witchcraft also stemmed from her connection to the night, darkness, and the underworld, as witches were believed to possess supernatural powers during these mystical times.

Hecate was regarded as the goddess who presided over magical arts and rituals. She was believed to have the ability to unlock the mysteries of the universe, granting access to hidden knowledge and supernatural powers. People would invoke her during magical rituals, seeking her guidance, protection, and assistance in their spellcasting and divination practices.

She was associated with transformation and shape-shifting, which were integral to many magical practices. It was believed that she could bestow the power of transformation upon her devotees, enabling them to assume different forms or change their appearances. This connection to transformation and shape-shifting made her particularly revered by those engaged in shamanic or shape-shifting practices.

Hecate's association with crossroads further enhanced her connection to magic and witchcraft. Crossroads were seen as magical and liminal spaces, where the boundaries between realms were thin. Hecate was believed to hold sway over these crossroads, and practitioners of magic would often perform rituals and spells at these intersections to harness her powers and gain access to hidden knowledge and otherworldly energies.

Those who sought Hecate's assistance in their magical endeavours would often make offerings to her. These offerings could include items such as honey, eggs, garlic, or other items associated with witchcraft and mysticism. Devotees would also engage in rituals, prayers, and incantations to invoke Hecate's presence and establish a strong connection with her.

Hecate's association with magic and witchcraft made her a revered figure among practitioners of the mystical arts in ancient Greece. Her knowledge, transformative abilities, and connection to liminal spaces made her an essential guide and ally for those seeking to tap into the realms of magic and supernatural power.

Mystery Cults:

Hecate's connections to the underworld and her role as a guide of souls were particularly significant in the realm of mystery cults and esoteric traditions. Hecate was often depicted as a guide of souls, assisting, and protecting the departed as they journeyed through the realm of the dead. She held the keys to the gates of the underworld, allowing her to traverse freely between the realms of the living and the dead. It was believed that she would guide and accompany souls during their transition from the physical world to the afterlife, ensuring their safe passage and offering them guidance along the way.

Hecate's role as a guide of souls aligned with various mystery cults, which were secretive religious organisations focused on the worship of specific deities and the exploration of hidden spiritual knowledge. These mystery cults often revolved around the themes of death, rebirth, and the afterlife. Initiates into these cults would undergo rituals and ceremonies that aimed to reveal the mysteries of existence and provide spiritual enlightenment. Hecate's association with the underworld and her role as a guide of souls made her an important figure within these cults.

One of the most famous mystery cults in ancient Greece was the Eleusinian Mysteries, centred around the worship of Demeter and Persephone. Hecate was often invoked in conjunction with these mysteries due to her connections with the underworld. She was seen as a supportive presence, aiding Demeter in her search for Persephone and offering guidance and protection during the initiatory experiences of the participants.

Hecate was also known as a psychopomp, a deity who guided souls to their final resting place. As a psychopomp, she not only guided souls to the underworld but also acted as a mediator between the realms of the living and the dead. Her role was to facilitate the transition of the soul and ensure its proper placement in the afterlife.

In the context of mystery cults and esoteric traditions, devotees of Hecate would engage in rituals and ceremonies aimed at establishing a connection with the underworld and the realm of the dead. Offerings would be made to Hecate to honour her as a guide of souls and to seek her assistance in matters related to the afterlife and spiritual transformation.

Syncretism and Hellenistic Influence:

The syncretism and Hellenistic influences on Hecate played a significant role in shaping her mythology, symbolism, and cult practices. During the Hellenistic period, there was a blending of Greek and Egyptian cultures, leading to syncretism between Greek deities and their Egyptian counterparts. Hecate, with her association with magic and her role as a protector, was often identified with the Egyptian goddesses Isis and Serapis. This syncretism expanded Hecate's attributes and symbolism, incorporating elements from Egyptian mythology and practices.

The Hellenistic period also saw the influence of Persian culture and religion. Hecate was sometimes associated with the Persian goddess Anahita, who represented water, fertility, and healing. This syncretism expanded Hecate's associations with fertility and nurturance, emphasising her role as a goddess of life-giving forces.

Mystery cults, which focused on secret initiations and rituals, were prevalent during the Hellenistic period. Hecate became associated with certain mystery cults, particularly those centred around the worship of Demeter and Persephone. In these cults, Hecate played a role as a guide and companion to Persephone in the underworld. This added a mystical and initiatory dimension to Hecate's mythology and worship.

The Hellenistic period also contributed to the development of Hecate's triple form as the Maiden, Mother, and Crone. This triadic aspect was influenced by the Hellenistic fascination with triads and the incorporation of multiple aspects of feminine power and wisdom into a unified goddess figure. Hecate's triple form symbolised the cycles of life, death, and rebirth, as well as the stages of a woman's life.

Hecate's connections to magic, witchcraft, and the occult were further emphasised during the Hellenistic period. She was regarded as a powerful sorceress and the mistress of spells, potions, and charms. Her associations with the moon, crossroads, and nocturnal activities made her an ideal figure for practitioners of magic and mystical arts.

Hecate's cult practices became more established and structured during the Hellenistic period. Temples and sanctuaries dedicated to Hecate were constructed, and specific rituals and ceremonies were developed to honour her. These practices included offerings of food, libations, and other gifts, as well as the performance of hymns and prayers.

Hecate's role in religious practices and cults exemplifies her multifaceted nature and the diverse ways in which people sought her guidance, protection, and mystical powers. From personal devotion and household rituals to public festivals and involvement in mystery cults, Hecate's worship and cult practices provided a means for individuals to connect with the divine, explore hidden realms, and seek empowerment in their lives.

Hecate's association with witchcraft, sorcery, and magic.

Hecate is closely associated with witchcraft, sorcery, and magic in Greek mythology. Her role as a goddess of magic and her association with the supernatural are prominent aspects of her character. Here are some points to consider regarding Hecate's connection to witchcraft, sorcery, and magic:

Patroness of Witchcraft:

Hecate is widely revered as the patroness of witchcraft and the occult in various spiritual and magical traditions. Here are more details about her connection to witchcraft and her role as a patron:

In ancient Greece, Hecate was associated with magic, witchcraft, and the practice of the occult arts. She was regarded as the goddess who had knowledge of secret spells, charms, and herbal remedies. People sought her assistance in matters related to divination, necromancy, and other forms of magic.

In ancient Greece, witchcraft was viewed as a mystical and powerful practice. It involved the manipulation of natural forces, the invocation of deities, and the use of spells and potions. Hecate, with her association with magic and her knowledge of occult arts, became closely linked with practitioners of witchcraft.

Hecate was believed to be a patroness and protector of witches. Those who practiced witchcraft would often invoke Hecate's aid and guidance in their magical workings. They would set up altars or shrines dedicated to Hecate and offer her offerings as a sign of devotion and respect.

Hecate's symbols, such as the torch, the key, the serpent, and the cauldron, are all closely associated with witchcraft and the occult. The torch represents the illumination of hidden knowledge, the key symbolises access to the mysteries of the unseen realms, the serpent represents transformation and wisdom, and the cauldron is a vessel of magical transformation and manifestation.

Hecate's association with crossroads, which are considered liminal and magical spaces, further solidifies her connection to witchcraft. In ancient Greece, witches were believed to gather at crossroads during the night to perform their rituals and commune with Hecate. These crossroads were seen as gateways to other realms and places of power.

In modern witchcraft and neopagan practices, Hecate continues to be revered as a patroness of witchcraft. Many modern witches draw inspiration from Hecate's energy and incorporate her symbols and rituals into their magical workings. They seek her guidance and assistance in their spiritual and magical practices, viewing her as a powerful ally and source of wisdom.

Magical Abilities:

Hecate is associated with various magical abilities and powers in Greek mythology and folklore. She is known as a powerful sorceress and a mistress of witchcraft. She possesses deep knowledge of spells, charms, and potions, and is skilled in the use of magical rituals and incantations. It is believed that she can bestow magical powers upon her devotees and assist them in their own magical practices.

Hecate is associated with the realm of divination and prophecy. She has the ability to see into the future and has knowledge of hidden things. She can provide insights, guidance, and revelations through various divinatory methods, such as tarot reading, scrying, or dream interpretation.

Hecate has a close connection to the realm of the dead and is considered a guide of souls. She possesses the ability to communicate with spirits and the deceased. It is believed that she can assist in contacting and communing with the spirits of departed loved ones or seeking guidance from ancestral spirits.

She is often depicted as a shape-shifter, able to assume various forms, including that of animals such as dogs, snakes, or owls. This ability represents her transformative nature and her ability to traverse different realms and dimensions.

Hecate is associated with healing and the use of herbs for medicinal purposes. She has knowledge of the healing properties of plants and the creation of herbal remedies. It is believed that she can provide guidance on herbalism and assist in physical and spiritual healing.

She is revered as a protective deity, particularly against evil spirits, negative energies, and malevolent magic. She is believed to have the power to banish and ward off harmful influences and to offer spiritual protection to her devotees.

Crossroads Magic:

Crossroads magic is closely associated with Hecate and holds a significant place in her mythology and worship.

Crossroads are considered liminal spaces, meaning they exist at the intersection of two or more realms or dimensions. They are seen as places of transition, where different energies converge and opportunities for transformation and magical workings arise. Hecate is often associated with liminality, and crossroads serve as a fitting setting for her worship and magical practices.

Crossroads are viewed as gateways to other realms, including the spirit world, the underworld, and realms of magic and mystery. Hecate, being a goddess with connections to the realm of the dead and the mysteries of the night, is believed to have the ability to navigate these realms and act as a guide for those seeking to cross between them.

Crossroads have long been associated with divination and decision making. In ancient times, individuals would seek Hecate's guidance and insight at crossroads to aid them in making important choices and receiving messages from the divine. Hecate is considered a wise and insightful deity who can offer clarity and direction in times of uncertainty.

Crossroads are often chosen as the location for offering rituals and invocations to Hecate. Devotees would bring offerings such as food, wine, herbs, or other symbolic items to the crossroads, placing them on altars or at the centre of the crossroads as a gesture of devotion. Invocations and prayers are performed to call upon Hecate's presence and seek her blessings and assistance.

Crossroads are also associated with protective magic, and Hecate is revered as a guardian and protector. It is believed that by invoking Hecate at crossroads, one can gain her protection against negative energies, evil spirits, and malevolent forces. Offerings and rituals at the crossroads are seen as acts of devotion that strengthen the bond between the practitioner and Hecate, ensuring her continued protection and guidance.

Crossroads magic in connection with Hecate is a powerful and transformative practice. It allows individuals to tap into the energy of liminality, seek guidance from the divine, and perform rituals and spells to manifest their intentions and desires. The crossroads serve as a sacred space where the mundane and the spiritual intersect, offering a gateway to the realm of magic and the mysteries of Hecate.

Necromancy:

Hecate has a strong association with the realm of the dead and necromancy. In Greek mythology, Hecate is often depicted as a guide of souls, leading them from the realm of the living to the realm of the dead. She is believed to have the ability to traverse between different realms and act as a mediator between the living and the deceased. As a psychopomp, she guides souls on their journey and ensures safe passage to the underworld.

She has strong connections with the underworld and is considered a powerful figure in its realm. While Hades is typically regarded as the ruler of the underworld, Hecate is often depicted as an influential and respected figure in this realm. Her association with the underworld further emphasises her connection to death, the afterlife, and the mysteries that lie beyond.

Hecate's association with the realm of the dead makes her closely tied to necromancy, which is the practice of communicating with the spirits of the deceased. In ancient Greece, individuals would seek Hecate's assistance in performing necromantic rituals, which involved contacting and seeking guidance from deceased ancestors or spirits. Hecate's role as a guide and mediator between realms made her an important deity in such practices.

Hecate is often invoked and honoured in rituals and ceremonies dedicated to the dead. People would offer food, libations, and other symbolic items at crossroads or other sacred places associated with Hecate, as a means of honouring and appeasing the spirits of the deceased. These offerings were believed to strengthen the connection between the living and the dead, and Hecate was seen as a facilitator of this connection.

Hecate's association with the realm of the dead also extends to her role as a protector against malevolent spirits and entities. It was believed that Hecate possessed the power to ward off harmful influences from the underworld and could be invoked for protection against restless spirits or negative energies. Her presence and offerings were thought to create a barrier of protection for those who sought her aid.

Protective Magic:

Hecate is closely linked with protective magic in various mythological and magical traditions. She is often invoked as a guardian and protector against evil forces, malevolent spirits, and negative energies. Her presence is believed to create a shield of protection around individuals and their surroundings. She is regarded as a powerful ally in banishing and warding off harmful influences, including psychic attacks, curses, and the evil eye.

Hecate's role as a guardian extends to the establishment of magical boundaries. She is invoked to set up protective barriers around homes, temples, altars, or other sacred spaces. People would seek her assistance in creating energetic shields, invoking her presence to ward off unwanted influences and maintain a sacred and safe environment.

She is revered as a patroness of witchcraft and is closely associated with spellcasting and magical rituals. She is believed to bestow magical abilities and knowledge upon her devotees, empowering them to practice protective magic. Witches and practitioners often call upon Hecate's aid to enhance the effectiveness of their spells and to provide guidance in matters of magical protection.

Hecate's symbols, such as keys, torches, serpents, and crescent moons, are often incorporated into amulets and talismans for protection. These items are believed to carry Hecate's energy and serve as powerful protective charms. They are worn or kept in sacred spaces to ward off negative influences and to invoke Hecate's guidance and blessings.

Hecate's association with protective magic showcases her role as a guardian and defender against harmful forces. Her presence is believed to create a shield of protection, offering assistance to those who seek her aid in warding off evil, maintaining energetic boundaries, and practicing effective magic.

Ritual Offerings and Practices:

Those seeking Hecate's favour would often make offerings to her as part of their magical practices. Individuals would perform devotional rituals dedicated to Hecate to establish a connection and seek her favour. These rituals may include offerings, prayers, invocations, and specific actions or gestures to honour her.

Hecate is closely associated with crossroads, so performing rituals at crossroads is a common practice. People would gather at a crossroads, usually at night, and invoke Hecate's presence through offerings, chants, and prayers.

Hecate's connection with the moon makes lunar rituals significant in her worship. Observing rituals during specific lunar phases, such as the new moon or full moon, is believed to enhance the connection with Hecate and amplify the effectiveness of the rituals.

Lighting candles, particularly black or purple ones, is a common offering made to Hecate. The flame represents her torch and symbolises illumination, transformation, and guidance.

Burning incense, especially those with earthy or mystical scents like myrrh, frankincense, or patchouli, is a popular offering. The rising smoke is believed to carry prayers and offerings to the divine realm.

Offering herbs and plants associated with Hecate, such as mugwort, lavender, mandrake, or rue, can be made. These plants are believed to have protective and magical properties.

Offerings of food and drink are also made to Hecate. This may include offerings of honey, pomegranates, garlic, eggs, or bread. These offerings symbolise abundance, nourishment, and sustenance.

Offering symbolic keys to Hecate represents opening the doors to her realm and inviting her presence into one's life.

Seeking guidance from Hecate through divination practices, such as tarot readings, scrying, or oracle cards, is common. Hecate is considered a patroness of divination, and practitioners may ask for her insights and wisdom in matters of personal growth, decision-making, or spiritual development.

Practicing meditation and pathworking to connect with Hecate's energy and seek her guidance is another approach. Individuals may visualise themselves journeying through the underworld or walking a path illuminated by Hecate's torch, seeking her insights and blessings.

Hecate is believed to communicate through dreams. Engaging in dream work, such as keeping a dream journal, setting intentions before sleep, and seeking Hecate's guidance in dreams, can be a way to connect with her.

These rituals, offerings, and practices are performed with reverence and sincerity to establish a connection with Hecate, seek her favour, and invite her guidance and blessings into one's life. They demonstrate devotion and a desire to cultivate a meaningful relationship with the goddess of magic, witchcraft, and the crossroads.

Chapter 4. Hecate as a Triple Goddess.

Hecate is often depicted and understood as a triple goddess, embodying the three-fold aspect of Maiden, Mother, and Crone. This tripartite nature symbolises the different stages of a woman's life and the cyclical nature of existence. Here's a closer look at each aspect:

Maiden:

The Maiden aspect represents youth, innocence, and the potential for growth and new beginnings. As the Maiden, Hecate is associated with vitality, independence, and the blossoming of life. She embodies the qualities of curiosity, exploration, and the pursuit of knowledge. The Maiden aspect of Hecate is often depicted as a young woman, full of energy and enthusiasm. Hecate as the maiden represents the youthful, innocent, and potential aspects of her archetype. Here are some details about Hecate as the maiden and her associations with youth, innocence, and the potential for growth and new beginnings:

As the maiden, Hecate embodies the energy and vitality of youth. She is often depicted as a young and vibrant goddess, symbolising the freshness and enthusiasm that comes with new beginnings. This aspect of Hecate represents the youthful spirit within all of us, reminding us of the endless possibilities and excitement that accompany the early stages of life's journeys.

Hecate as the maiden represents a state of purity and innocence. In this form, she is untouched by the experiences and challenges of life. This innocence is not naive but rather carries a sense of openness, curiosity, and receptivity to new experiences and knowledge. Hecate as the maiden encourages us to approach life with a childlike wonder, embracing the unknown and remaining open to the lessons and growth it brings.

The maiden aspect of Hecate signifies the potential for growth and development. Like the budding of a flower or the sprouting of a seed, the maiden embodies the potential waiting to be nurtured and cultivated. Hecate as the maiden inspires us to embrace new beginnings, take risks, and explore uncharted territories. She encourages us to tap into our creativity, follow our passions, and step outside of our comfort zones to unlock our full potential.

Hecate as the maiden signifies the readiness for new beginnings and fresh starts. She symbolises the transition from one phase of life to another, whether it be embarking on a new project, starting a new relationship, or beginning a new chapter in one's personal growth.

Mother:

The Mother aspect of Hecate is often depicted as a mature woman, embodying the nurturing and loving qualities associated with motherhood. Hecate as the mother represents the nurturing, protective, and generative aspects of her archetype. Here are some details about Hecate as the mother and her associations with maternal qualities:

As the mother, Hecate embodies the qualities of nurturing and protection. She is often depicted as a caring and compassionate figure, guiding, and supporting those in need. Hecate's maternal energy is nurturing and comforting, offering solace and strength to those who seek her aid. She provides a safe space for growth and healing, like a mother providing a nurturing environment for her children.

Hecate as the mother represents fertility and the generative power of creation. She is associated with the cycles of life, birth, and growth. In this aspect, she is connected to the abundance of the Earth and the natural world. Hecate's motherly energy inspires creativity and the birthing of new ideas, projects, and life experiences. She encourages us to embrace our own creative potential and to honour the cycles of growth and transformation.

The mother aspect of Hecate embodies wisdom and guidance. Like a wise mother, she offers counsel, insight, and support. Hecate's maternal energy carries the wisdom gained through experience and the ability to provide guidance in navigating life's challenges. She encourages us to trust our instincts, listen to our inner voice, and make choices that align with our highest good. Hecate's motherly presence reminds us of the importance of self-care, self-love, and nurturing our own well-being.

Hecate as the mother is also associated with protection and the establishment of boundaries. Like a vigilant guardian, she safeguards her devotees from harm and negativity. Hecate's maternal energy is protective, creating a shield of strength and resilience. She teaches us the importance of setting healthy boundaries and standing up for ourselves and our loved ones. By invoking Hecate as the mother, we can tap into her nurturing, protective, and wise energy to navigate life's challenges and foster a sense of security and well-being.

Crone:

The Crone aspect represents wisdom, maturity, and the waning phase of life. As the Crone, Hecate embodies wisdom, introspection, and the transformative power of age and experience. She is associated with the mysteries of life, death, and rebirth. The Crone aspect of Hecate is often depicted as an elderly woman, representing the culmination of knowledge and the depth of understanding that comes with age.

As the crone, Hecate embodies wisdom gained through a lifetime of experiences. She is a symbol of deep insight, intuitive knowing, and profound understanding. Hecate's crone energy represents the culmination of knowledge acquired over time. She invites us to embrace our own wisdom and tap into the depth of our inner knowing. Hecate's crone aspect encourages us to seek wisdom, learn from our experiences, and grow in our understanding of ourselves and the world.

The crone aspect of Hecate is closely associated with transformation and the natural cycles of life. Just as autumn leads to winter, the crone represents the stage of life where one's journey approaches its end. Hecate's crone energy teaches us to embrace the transformative power of endings and to find strength in the process of letting go. She guides us through transitions, helping us navigate the path of transformation and find new beginnings within the endings.

Hecate as the crone is strongly connected to magic and the mystical realms. She is a guardian of ancient knowledge, hidden wisdom, and the mysteries of the unseen. Hecate's crone energy invites us to delve into the depths of the unknown, to explore the mysteries of life, and to embrace our own innate magical abilities. She guides us in working with spells, rituals, divination, and other forms of magical practice. Hecate's crone aspect reminds us of the power and potential that lie within us, waiting to be tapped into.

The crone aspect of Hecate encourages us to embrace our shadow selves and engage in shadow work. She teaches us that true wisdom comes from accepting and integrating all aspects of ourselves, including the parts that may be considered dark or hidden. Hecate's crone energy supports us in exploring our deepest fears, wounds, and patterns, and helps us transform them into sources of strength and healing. Through shadow work, we can uncover hidden aspects of ourselves and grow in self-awareness and self-empowerment.

The Maiden, Mother, and Crone aspects of Hecate emphasise the multifaceted nature of femininity and the diverse roles that women play in society and in the greater cosmic order. They remind us of the importance of embracing and honouring each phase of life, recognising the inherent wisdom and beauty within each stage.

Significance of the triple form and its representation in mythology and worship

The triple form of Hecate holds significant meaning and is represented in various ways in mythology and worship. Here are some key points regarding the significance of Hecate's triple form and its representation:

Symbol of Completeness:

The triple form of Hecate is a prominent aspect of her mythology and worship. From her portrayal as the maiden, mother, and crone, to her associations with the three realms of earth, sea, and sky, Hecate's triple form represents the encompassing nature of existence. It embodies the cycles of life, the balance of energies, and the wholeness of the divine feminine.

Hecate's triple form as the maiden, mother, and crone represents the full spectrum of womanhood and the completeness of the feminine archetype. It encompasses the stages of life, from birth to maturity to the wisdom gained through aging. Hecate's triple form also reflects the interconnectedness and harmony of the natural world, as it encompasses the three realms of earth, sea, and sky. The triple form symbolises the cyclical nature of existence, the balance of energies, and the integration of different aspects of being.

In worship and devotion, Hecate's triple form is honoured as a symbol of completeness. It reminds us of the multidimensional nature of the divine feminine and invites us to embrace all aspects of ourselves. By recognising and honouring the triple form of Hecate, we acknowledge the importance of growth, nurturing, wisdom, and the interconnectedness of life's cycles. Through the understanding of her triple form, we can find inspiration and guidance in our own journeys of self-discovery, transformation, and spiritual evolution.

Connection to the Moon:

One of the significant associations of Hecate's triple form is with the phases of the moon. The moon's cyclical journey through its various phases mirrors the transformative nature of Hecate and the triple aspects of the goddess. Each phase of the moon corresponds to a specific aspect of Hecate's triple form, further enriching the symbolism and representation of her divine nature.

Goddess of Crossroads:

Hecate's triple form is closely linked to her role as the goddess of crossroads, which are seen as liminal spaces where different paths converge and choices are made. In this context, her triple form represents the various paths and possibilities that individuals encounter in their lives, highlighting the significance of choices and the transformative nature of decision-making.

The maiden aspect of Hecate, representing youth, innocence, and new beginnings, aligns with the path of potentiality and exploration. Just as the maiden embarks on a journey of self-discovery and growth, individuals standing at the crossroads of life's choices embody the maiden's energy. They are filled with curiosity, optimism, and the excitement of embarking on a new path. The maiden aspect of Hecate guides them to embrace possibilities and step into new experiences with enthusiasm.

The mother aspect of Hecate embodies nurturing, abundance, and the fruition of choices. At the crossroads, individuals who have made choices and committed to a particular path align with the mother's energy. They nourish and nurture their chosen path, investing their time, energy, and resources to bring their visions to life. The mother aspect of Hecate supports and empowers them as they navigate the challenges and joys that arise along their chosen path.

The crone aspect of Hecate, symbolising wisdom, guidance, and transformation, reveals herself to individuals who have reached a point of transition or reflection at the crossroads. These individuals stand at a juncture where they can make significant changes, release old patterns, and embark on a new path. The crone aspect of Hecate offers her guidance, encouraging deep introspection, and providing the wisdom needed to make informed choices. She reminds them that even in times of uncertainty, there is great potential for personal growth and transformation.

Mythological Depictions:

Hecate's triple form is often depicted in various mythological stories and artworks, showcasing her multifaceted nature and the depth of her powers. In some representations, Hecate is shown with three faces or three distinct forms, each representing a different aspect of her divine essence. These depictions highlight the symbolic significance of her triple form and its representation in mythology and worship.

Three Faces of Hecate - One of the prominent depictions of Hecate's triple form is the portrayal of her with three faces, also known as the "triple-headed Hecate." Each face represents a distinct phase of the moon and symbolises the threefold aspects of her goddesshood: maiden, mother, and crone. The maiden face embodies youth, curiosity, and new beginnings, while the mother face represents nurturing, abundance, and growth. The crone face signifies wisdom, transformation, and the mysteries of the underworld. This triple-headed depiction emphasises Hecate's connection to lunar phases and her embodiment of the cyclical nature of life.

Three Forms of Hecate - In other representations, Hecate is depicted with three distinct forms, often associated with her association with the three realms: earth, sea, and sky. The earthly form represents her connection to the physical realm and the natural world. The watery form symbolises her dominion over the depths of the sea and the mysteries that lie within. The ethereal form represents her connection to the celestial realm and the cosmic forces that govern the universe. These three forms of Hecate showcase her universal presence and her ability to traverse different realms.

Throughout history, various artists have captured Hecate's triple form in their artworks, whether through sculptures, paintings, or other mediums. These artistic representations often depict Hecate in her triple aspect, showcasing her three faces or three distinct forms. Such artworks not only serve as visual representations of her triple form but also evoke a sense of her power, mystery, and transformative nature.

They inspire reverence and contemplation, inviting viewers to delve deeper into the symbolism and significance of Hecate's triple form.

The depiction of Hecate's triple form in mythology and art serves as a powerful symbol of her multifaceted nature and the encompassing influence she holds over various aspects of life. It embodies the concept of completeness, encompassing the past, present, and future, as well as the different stages of life and the cyclical nature of existence.

Mystical and Magical Power:

Hecate's triple form holds great significance in mystical and magical practices, where her triple aspect is revered and invoked for its potent symbolism and transformative energies. Across various esoteric traditions, Hecate's triple form is seen as a source of profound wisdom, intuitive guidance, and magical power. Let's explore how her triple form is revered and utilised in mystical and magical practices.

Hecate's triple form is often associated with the concept of the Triple Goddess, a powerful archetype found in many spiritual and mystical traditions. As the Maiden, Mother, and Crone, Hecate embodies the three stages of a woman's life, representing the cycles of youth, maturity, and wisdom. In mystical practices, this symbolism is embraced to connect with the different aspects of the divine feminine and to invoke Hecate's transformative energies for personal growth, healing, and spiritual development.

Practitioners of mystical and magical traditions often invoke Hecate's triple form in rituals and ceremonies to seek her guidance, protection, and assistance in their spiritual work. The three faces or forms of Hecate are called upon to aid in divination, spellcasting, energy work, and astral travel. Each face or form is believed to hold specific attributes and powers that can be harnessed for various magical endeavours. Devotees may create altars or sacred spaces dedicated to Hecate's triple form, adorned with symbols and objects representing each aspect of her divine nature.

Hecate's triple form is particularly revered in the realm of transformation and shadow work. Her association with the underworld and her role as a guide of souls aligns her with the depths of the human psyche and the exploration of hidden aspects of the self. In mystical and magical practices, invoking Hecate's triple form can assist in uncovering and integrating shadow aspects, facilitating personal growth, and embracing the transformative power of self-discovery.

Ritual Tools and Symbols:

In mystical and magical practices, specific ritual tools and symbols are often associated with Hecate's triple form. These may include triple-faced statues or images, triple moon symbols, triple-wicked candles, or wands with three branches or points. These objects are used to connect with Hecate's triple energies and to channel her transformative and magical powers in rituals and spell work.

The reverence of Hecate's triple form in mystical and magical practices speaks to the profound symbolism and power it holds within these traditions. By invoking her triple aspect, practitioners seek alignment with the cycles of life, embrace the transformative nature of the self, and tap into the intuitive wisdom and magical energies associated with Hecate. Her triple form serves as a focal point for personal empowerment, spiritual growth, and the manifestation of intentions in mystical and magical practices.

Hecate's connection to lunar phases and cycles

Hecate is often referred to as the lunar goddess, and her connection to the moon is a prominent feature of her character. Throughout mythology and worship, Hecate's association with the moon is deeply intertwined with her role as a powerful and mystical deity. Let's explore Hecate's connection to lunar phases and cycles and the significance it holds in understanding her character and influence.

The Lunar Goddess:

Hecate's identification as a lunar goddess stem from her close association with the moon and its various phases. In ancient Greek mythology, the moon was seen as a symbol of feminine power and mystery, and Hecate embodied these qualities in her divine nature. As the lunar goddess, Hecate holds sway over the ebb and flow of the moon's energy and the mystical properties it represents.

Symbolism of the Moon:

The moon symbolises a multitude of concepts, including cycles, renewal, intuition, magic, and the subconscious. These attributes align closely with Hecate's domain and her role as a goddess of magic, witchcraft, and the mysteries of the night. The moon's cyclical nature reflects the ever-changing aspects of Hecate's triple form and the transformative energies she embodies.

Moon Phases and Hecate's Influence:

Hecate's connection to the moon extends beyond its overall symbolism. Each phase of the moon holds a distinct energy and meaning, and Hecate's influence can be seen in relation to these phases:

New Moon: The new moon represents beginnings, potential, and setting intentions. Hecate's association with the new moon highlights her role as a guide and guardian of new beginnings, offering support and assistance in initiating transformative journeys.

Waxing Moon: As the moon grows in illumination, it signifies growth, abundance, and manifestation. During this phase, Hecate's influence can be invoked to harness the energy of growth, pursue goals, and amplify desires.

Full Moon: The full moon is a time of heightened energy, illumination, and the culmination of intentions. Hecate's connection to the full moon aligns with her role as a goddess of magic and witchcraft, as this phase is considered potent for spell work, divination, and deepening spiritual connections.

Waning Moon: As the moon diminishes in illumination, it represents release, letting go, and banishing. Hecate's association with the waning moon reflects her role as a guide through transitions and the release of what no longer serves, allowing for personal transformation and renewal.

By understanding Hecate's connection to lunar phases and cycles, we gain insight into her role as a deity of transformation, magic, and the mysteries of the night. Her alignment with the moon's energies allows individuals to work with her in various spiritual practices, seeking her guidance, protection, and empowerment throughout the lunar cycle.

The Waxing Moon: Maiden Aspect

In her maiden aspect, Hecate embodies the waxing moon phase. The waxing moon represents new beginnings, growth, and potential. Just as the moon increases in illumination, Hecate's maiden aspect signifies youth, innocence, and the potential for new beginnings. As the maiden, Hecate brings forth the energy of freshness, enthusiasm, and the anticipation of what is to come. She is associated with youthful vitality, exploration, and the pursuit of new paths and opportunities.

As the moon transitions from darkness to illumination during the waxing phase, Hecate embodies the energy of emergence, expansion, and the unfolding of possibilities. Let's explore Hecate's connection to the Waxing Moon and the significance it holds in her mythology and worship.

Just as the Waxing Moon grows in illumination, Hecate's association with this lunar phase represents the concept of growth and new beginnings. The Waxing Moon is a time of increasing energy, where intentions are set, plans are put into motion, and new opportunities arise. Hecate, in her role as the goddess of potential, channels this energy and inspires individuals to embrace growth, pursue their aspirations, and embark on new ventures. She is a beacon of light guiding individuals along their chosen paths, encouraging them to step into their power and embrace the transformative potential of new beginnings.

The Waxing Moon is often associated with fertility and creative energy. It is a time when ideas take shape, projects gain momentum, and the spark of inspiration ignites. Hecate's connection to the Waxing Moon amplifies this creative energy and encourages individuals to tap into their innate abilities, unleash their creativity, and give birth to new endeavours. She is the patroness of artistic expression, encouraging individuals to explore their passions, embrace their unique talents, and manifest their creative visions.

In many mythological stories, Hecate is depicted as the initiator, guiding individuals through rites of passage and initiating them into new phases of life. Just as the Waxing Moon initiates the lunar cycle, Hecate's association with this phase signifies the initiation of new paths, experiences, and personal growth. She offers her wisdom and guidance to those who are embarking on new journeys, helping them navigate the challenges and embrace the opportunities that lie ahead. Hecate's presence during the Waxing Moon serves as a reminder that growth and transformation are inherent aspects of life's journey.

During the Waxing Moon, individuals can seek Hecate's influence and guidance to harness the energy of growth, new beginnings, and potential. This can be done through rituals, meditations, or simply connecting with her energy in a personal and intuitive way. Some practices that may be incorporated include lighting candles to symbolise the increasing illumination of the moon, setting intentions for growth and manifestation, and invoking Hecate's presence through prayers or invocations. By aligning oneself with Hecate's association to the Waxing Moon, individuals can tap into the fertile energy of creation and embark on a path of growth and new possibilities.

The Full Moon: Mother Aspect

Hecate's mother aspect aligns with the full moon, the peak of its illumination. The full moon symbolises abundance, fertility, and the culmination of intentions. As the mother, Hecate represents nurturing, protection, and the realisation of desires. In her mother aspect, she embodies the energy of fulfilment, wisdom, and the power to manifest one's goals. Hecate's role as the mother figure emphasises her nurturing and supportive nature, offering guidance and assistance in realising one's potential.

The Full Moon is a time of abundance and manifestation. As the moon shines in its full brilliance, it symbolises the culmination of energy and the realisation of desires. Hecate, in her association with the Full Moon, embodies the energy of abundance and the power to manifest one's intentions. She is the goddess of fulfilment, bestowing blessings upon those who seek her guidance. During the Full Moon phase, Hecate's energy flows freely, empowering individuals to tap into their own abundance and manifest their goals and aspirations. By invoking Hecate during the Full Moon, individuals can align themselves with the energy of abundance and harness the power of manifestation.

The Full Moon is a time of illumination and heightened insight. As the moon reaches its fullest potential, it radiates a powerful light that brings clarity and reveals hidden truths. Similarly, Hecate's association with the Full Moon emphasises her role as the goddess of illumination and wisdom. During this phase, Hecate's energy shines brightly, guiding individuals on their spiritual path and offering profound insight into their lives. By connecting with Hecate during the Full Moon, individuals can seek her wisdom, gain clarity, and access deep intuitive knowledge. It is a time to embrace Hecate's illuminating presence and invite her guidance into one's life.

The Full Moon represents the peak of the moon's power, and it is no different in Hecate's association with this lunar phase. Hecate, as the goddess of crossroads and transformation, is closely aligned with the energy of the Full Moon. It is during this phase that her transformative power is at its strongest. The Full Moon serves as a catalyst for change, urging individuals to embrace their personal power, release what no longer serves them, and embark on a path of growth and transformation. Hecate's presence during the Full Moon reminds us of our own inner strength and the potential for profound personal change. By invoking Hecate's energy and embracing her transformative power, individuals can navigate their own crossroads and undergo personal growth and evolution.

During the Full Moon phase, individuals can engage in rituals and practices to honour Hecate's connection to this powerful lunar phase. These rituals may include offerings and invocations to Hecate, divination practices to seek her guidance, spells for abundance and manifestation, or simply spending time in meditation and reflection under the moon's radiant light. By aligning oneself with Hecate's association with the Full Moon, individuals can tap into the heightened energy, embrace the potential for abundance and transformation, and seek the wisdom and guidance that Hecate offers.

The Full Moon holds a special place in Hecate's connection to lunar phases and cycles. It represents a time of abundance, illumination, and the peak of power. By honouring Hecate during this phase, individuals can align themselves with her transformative energy, manifest their desires, gain insight, and embark on a path of personal growth and evolution.

The Waning Moon: Crone Aspect

Hecate's crone aspect corresponds to the waning moon phase. The waning moon represents release, introspection, and the shedding of what no longer serves. In her crone aspect, Hecate embodies wisdom, introspection, and the transformative power of letting go. She guides individuals through the process of releasing old patterns, limiting beliefs, and aspects of themselves that no longer align with their highest good. Hecate's crone aspect holds the energy of transformation, renewal, and the wisdom gained through life's experiences.

By representing the three lunar phases, Hecate's triple form encompasses the entirety of the lunar cycle and reflects the cycles of life and personal growth. Her triple lunar goddess aspect serves as a powerful symbol of completeness, embracing the journey from initiation and new beginnings to fulfilment and transformation. It reminds individuals of the ever-changing nature of life and the cyclical patterns present in the universe.

The Waning Moon phase, which follows the Full Moon, holds a significant place in Hecate's connection to lunar phases and cycles. It signifies the transition from fullness to introspection and release. During this phase, Hecate's energy aligns with the waning lunar energy, representing the gradual decrease of light and the journey inward. Let's explore Hecate's association with the Waning Moon and how it symbolises introspection, release, and the power of transformation.

As the moon begins to wane, Hecate's connection to the Waning Moon invites individuals to turn their attention inward. It is a time for introspection, self-reflection, and deep inner work. Hecate, as the goddess of crossroads and transformation, guides individuals through this phase of the lunar cycle, encouraging them to delve into the depths of their emotions, thoughts, and experiences. By embracing Hecate's energy during the Waning Moon, individuals can embark on a journey of self-discovery, gaining insights into their inner landscape and uncovering hidden aspects of themselves.

The Waning Moon phase is a time for release and letting go. Just as the moon gradually diminishes in size, Hecate's association with the Waning Moon represents the power of release and surrender. It is an opportunity to shed what no longer serves us, whether it be negative emotions, outdated beliefs, or attachments that hinder personal growth. Hecate, as the goddess of crossroads, guides individuals in the process of releasing what no longer aligns with their path, allowing space for new beginnings. By invoking Hecate's energy during the Waning Moon, individuals can seek her guidance in the practice of letting go, freeing themselves from what weighs them down and embracing a sense of liberation and renewal.

The Waning Moon phase, with its focus on release and introspection, also holds the power of transformation and rebirth. Hecate's connection to this phase emphasises her role as a guide in the process of personal transformation. Just as the moon's light diminishes, giving way to darkness, Hecate guides individuals through their own periods of transition and growth. By embracing the energy of the Waning Moon and invoking Hecate's presence, individuals can harness the power of transformation, allowing the old to fade away and making space for the new to emerge. Hecate's energy during the Waning Moon encourages individuals to trust the process of transformation, knowing that through release and introspection, they can experience profound growth and rebirth.

During the Waning Moon phase, individuals can engage in rituals and practices to honour Hecate's connection to this transformative lunar phase. These may include rituals of release, such as writing down what needs to be let go and burning or burying the paper, meditation, and introspection to gain clarity and insight, or working with Hecate's symbols and tools, such as her torch or keys, as a representation of unlocking and releasing. By aligning with Hecate's association with the Waning Moon, individuals can tap into the transformative energy of this phase, embrace the power of release, and invite positive change and rebirth into their lives.

Lunar Magic and Divination:

Hecate's association with lunar phases extends to the realm of magical and divinatory practices. Followers of Hecate often perform rituals, spells, and divination during specific lunar phases, harnessing the energy of the moon to enhance their magical workings and seek guidance from the goddess. Let's explore Hecate's connection to lunar magic and divination and how her followers incorporate the power of the moon into their spiritual practices.

Hecate's connection to lunar phases provides her followers with a potent framework for magical timing. Each lunar phase holds its own unique energy and symbolism, and followers of Hecate align their rituals and spells with specific phases to enhance their intentions and manifestations. For example, during the Waxing Moon, when the moon is growing in illumination, practitioners may focus on spells and rituals for growth, abundance, and new beginnings. Conversely, during the Waning Moon, when the moon is diminishing, rituals of release, banishing, and divination may be performed. By attuning to the different lunar phases, followers of Hecate can optimise their magical workings and work in harmony with the natural cycles of the moon.

Lunar phases provide a powerful backdrop for rituals and spells dedicated to Hecate. During the Waxing Moon, followers may invoke Hecate's energy to manifest their desires, perform abundance rituals, or seek her assistance in matters of growth and opportunity. They may light candles, charge crystals, and recite incantations to harness Hecate's transformative power. Conversely, during the Waning Moon, rituals of release, banishing, and inner exploration are performed. Followers may seek Hecate's guidance in letting go of what no longer serves them, purging negative energy, or embarking on a journey of self-discovery. These rituals and spells not only align with the lunar phases but also serve as a way to connect with Hecate's energy and invite her presence into their magical practice.

Divination is another practice closely associated with Hecate's worship and the lunar phases. The moon, with its mystical and ever-changing nature, is seen as a conduit for intuitive insight and divine messages. Followers of Hecate may perform divination rituals during specific lunar phases to seek guidance, gain clarity, and tap into their own intuitive wisdom. They may use tools such as tarot cards, runes, scrying mirrors, or other divinatory methods to connect with the lunar energy and receive messages from Hecate. The different phases of the moon are believed to influence the quality of divination, with the Waxing Moon amplifying potential and opportunity, and the Waning Moon offering insight into release and transformation. By engaging in divination during specific lunar phases, followers of Hecate can deepen their connection with the goddess and receive guidance on their spiritual journey.

Hecate's association with lunar phases and cycles provides a powerful framework for magical and divinatory practices. Her followers honour and work with the energy of the moon, aligning their rituals, spells, and divination with specific lunar phases. By attuning to the waxing and waning energy of the moon, practitioners can optimise their magical workings, seek Hecate's guidance, and tap into their own intuitive wisdom.

Chapter 5: Hecate as the Goddess of Crossroads.

Crossroads held significant symbolism and importance in ancient Greek culture. They were seen as sacred and liminal spaces, where different paths intersected, and choices were made. Here are some key aspects regarding the symbolism and importance of crossroads:

Liminality and Transitions:

Crossroads, in ancient times, held profound significance as liminal spaces—a concept rooted in the idea of being in-between or on the threshold. These crossroads were considered sacred, not merely as physical intersections of roads, but as symbolic gateways connecting different realms and states of being.

Liminal spaces, such as crossroads, were viewed as places of transition, where one could move from one phase of life to another, or from one realm to another. They embodied the liminal state, a state of in-betweenness where boundaries blur, and transformation becomes possible.

Hecate, as the Goddess of Crossroads, embodies this liminality and the transformative power that resides within it. She is the guardian and guide of these threshold spaces, overseeing the transitions and the choices made at these crossroads. In her presence, one can navigate the liminal space and embrace the opportunities for growth and change that it offers.

Crossroads represented a meeting point of paths, symbolising the choices and decisions individuals face in their lives. They served as reminders that at every juncture, there are different directions one can take, and each choice leads to a unique outcome. Hecate's presence at the crossroads grants wisdom and guidance, helping seekers make informed decisions and navigate their chosen paths.

Furthermore, crossroads were not just physical locations but also metaphorical representations of pivotal moments in one's journey. They marked transitions from childhood to adulthood, from ignorance to knowledge, from one phase of life to the next. Hecate, as the Goddess of Crossroads, embodies the transformative power of these transitions, assisting individuals in embracing their growth and stepping into new phases of their lives.

In the liminal space of the crossroads, boundaries dissolve, and the veil between worlds becomes thin. This liminality allows for communion with unseen realms, making it a potent space for spiritual practices and divination. Hecate's association with the crossroads also extends to her role as a guide of souls, leading them through the liminal space between life and death.

Meeting of Divine and Human:

Crossroads were revered as sacred spaces where the realms of the divine and the human intersected. It was believed that gods, goddesses, and spirits frequented these liminal places, making them ideal locations for encounters with the divine, offerings, and rituals.

In ancient times, crossroads were considered a nexus point where the boundaries between the mortal realm and the realm of the gods were blurred. It was believed that these liminal spaces provided a meeting ground for both worlds, allowing for communication and interaction between the divine and the human.

The connection of crossroads with divine presence and activity can be traced back to the belief that these intersections were inhabited by spiritual entities. Hecate, as the Goddess of Crossroads, was believed to dwell in these sacred spaces, overseeing the passage between realms and serving as a mediator between mortals and the divine.

The presence of gods and spirits at crossroads made them auspicious locations for offering devotion and seeking divine favour. Individuals would often make offerings, such as food, flowers, and other symbolic items, at these crossroads to attract the attention and blessings of the gods. It was believed that the energy of the crossroads enhanced the connection between mortals and the divine, making prayers and petitions more potent.

Rituals and ceremonies were also performed at crossroads to honour the gods and invoke their presence. These rituals included purification rites, invocations, and the recitation of prayers. Seekers would come to these liminal spaces seeking divine guidance, wisdom, and protection, believing that the crossroads served as a gateway to the realms beyond.

Encountering the divine at crossroads was seen as a transformative experience, as it brought the human closer to the numinous and expanded their understanding of the interconnectedness of all things. The meeting of the divine and human realms at these sacred intersections held great significance in ancient religious practices, symbolising the bridging of worlds and the possibility of divine intervention in mortal affairs.

Magic and Rituals:

Crossroads held great significance in the realm of magic and rituals. They were considered places of power, where the boundaries between the mundane world and the spiritual realm were believed to be thin. This liminal space made crossroads ideal locations for performing magical workings, spells, and rituals.

Magical practitioners would often gather at crossroads to perform rituals and cast spells. They believed that the energy at crossroads amplified their magical intentions and facilitated communication with the divine. These rituals ranged from simple acts of devotion and offerings to complex ceremonies involving intricate spell work and incantations.

Offerings and sacrifices were made at crossroads to appease and gain the favour of deities, with Hecate being a primary recipient of such offerings. These offerings could include items such as food, wine, herbs, flowers, and symbolic objects associated with Hecate, such as keys or torches. The act of making an offering was seen as a form of communication and exchange with the divine, establishing a connection between the mortal and spiritual realms.

Spells and magical workings performed at crossroads often focused on a variety of intentions, including protection, purification, love, prosperity, and divination. The energy of the crossroads was believed to amplify the potency of these spells, enhancing their effectiveness. Practitioners would invoke Hecate's assistance in their magical endeavours, seeking her guidance, power, and blessings.

Divination practices were also common at crossroads. Individuals seeking insights into their future or guidance in making decisions would use various divinatory methods, such as reading omens, casting lots, or using tarot cards or other divination tools. Hecate, as a goddess associated with wisdom and knowledge, was often invoked during these divination rituals, with the crossroads serving as a sacred space for receiving messages and revelations.

Hecate as the guardian of crossroads and her role in guiding choices and paths

Hecate is often portrayed as the guardian of crossroads and is associated with guiding choices and paths. Her role in this regard highlights her importance as a goddess of transitions and decision-making. Here are some key points regarding Hecate's role as the guardian of crossroads and her guidance in choices and paths:

Hecate is revered as a protector of travellers, particularly at crossroads. In ancient times, crossroads were considered dangerous places, associated with uncertainty and potential harm. Hecate was believed to watch over those who traversed these liminal spaces, ensuring their safe passage and providing them with guidance and assistance on their chosen paths.

Hecate is sought after for her wisdom and guidance in decision-making. When individuals arrived at a crossroad, they would often invoke Hecate to aid them in making the right choice. She was believed to possess knowledge of the past, present, and future, enabling her to provide insight and foresight to those who sought her counsel. Hecate's guidance helped individuals navigate the complexities of their lives and make choices aligned with their highest good.

Hecate was associated with divination and oracular practices, further accentuating her role as a guide in choices and paths. At crossroads, individuals would seek Hecate's assistance in interpreting signs, omens, and dreams, which were believed to provide guidance and direction. Hecate's connection to the unseen realms and her ability to traverse different realms made her an apt guide for those seeking answers and clarity.

Hecate's association with crossroads extended to initiation ceremonies and rituals. Initiates would often undergo rites of passage at crossroads, invoking Hecate's presence to facilitate their spiritual transformation and provide guidance as they embarked on a new phase of their lives. Hecate's presence during these rituals was believed to strengthen the initiates and help them navigate the challenges and choices that lay ahead.

Chapter 6: Hecate and the Underworld.

Hecate's association with the realm of the dead and the Underworld is a significant aspect of her mythology and symbolism. She holds a unique position as a goddess who embodies the liminal spaces between life and death, and her connections to the Underworld are multifaceted. Here are some key aspects of Hecate's association with the realm of the dead and the Underworld:

Guide of Souls:

Hecate is often depicted as a psychopomp, a guide of souls. She assists and safeguards individuals during their transition from the realm of the living to the realm of the dead. With her torches illuminating the way, she offers guidance and protection to ensure the safe passage of souls through the shadowy paths of the Underworld.

Underworld Goddess:

Hecate has a distinct presence and authority within the Underworld. While she is not the ruler of the Underworld like Hades, she is considered one of its prominent goddesses. Her role as a companion to Persephone, the Queen of the Underworld, and her involvement in various myths related to the realm of the dead emphasise her close connection to this domain.

Necromancy and Divination:

Hecate is associated with practices such as necromancy and divination, which involve communication with the spirits of the dead. Her knowledge of the Underworld and her ability to navigate its mysteries made her a patroness of these mystical arts. Through these practices, individuals sought to connect with the deceased and gain insight from the realm of the dead.

Rituals and Offerings:

Hecate was honoured in various rituals and offerings related to the realm of the dead. Ancient Greeks would leave offerings for her at crossroads or at the entrances to homes to seek her favour and protection in matters involving the spirits of the deceased. These rituals acknowledged Hecate's role as a mediator between the living and the dead and sought her assistance in matters related to the Underworld.

Her role as a psychopomp and guide of souls

Hecate's role as a psychopomp and guide of souls is a fascinating aspect of her mythology. In Greek mythology, Hecate held a unique position as a goddess who facilitated the transition of souls between the realms of the living and the dead. With her torches illuminating the way, she guided and protected those embarking on their journey into the underworld.

As a psychopomp, Hecate acted as a compassionate escort, aiding departed souls in navigating the shadowy paths of the afterlife. She possessed the knowledge and power to traverse the thresholds between worlds, leading souls across the boundaries that separated the mortal realm from the realm of Hades.

When individuals passed away, it was believed that Hecate would appear at their side, extending a guiding hand to lead them through the perilous realm of the dead. Her torches, shining brightly in the darkness, provided solace and reassurance, warding off malevolent spirits and ensuring safe passage to the underworld.

Hecate's connection with the liminal spaces, such as crossroads and boundaries, further emphasised her role as a psychopomp. Just as she guided the souls along their ethereal journey, she also presided over the crossroads, where choices and paths intersected. This connection signified her ability to navigate the transitions and liminal moments in life, both in the mortal realm and the realm beyond.

In the realm of mythology, Hecate's involvement as a psychopomp is exemplified in various tales. One notable example is her role in assisting Demeter, the goddess of agriculture, in her search for her daughter Persephone, who had been abducted by Hades. Hecate accompanied Demeter in her descent into the underworld and served as a guide, ensuring their safe return to the surface.

Hecate's role as a psychopomp not only demonstrated her power and connection to the realms beyond, but also showcased her compassionate nature. She provided solace and support to souls in their transition, offering them a steady presence and guiding light. Her multifaceted role as a goddess of crossroads, magic, and the underworld intertwines with her duties as a psychopomp, creating a rich tapestry of symbolism and significance.

In our modern understanding, Hecate's role as a psychopomp continues to inspire and resonate. She represents the guiding force that assists us through life's transitions, offering wisdom, protection, and the courage to navigate the unknown. Through her archetype, we can find comfort in the belief that, even in the face of death, there is a compassionate presence guiding us towards our next destination.

Hecate's role as a guide of souls is mentioned in various mythological accounts and traditions. One of the most notable instances is her involvement in the myth of Orpheus and his descent into the underworld to rescue his beloved wife, Eurydice.

Orpheaus's journey to the Underworld:

According to the myth, Orpheus, a renowned musician, and poet, ventured into the realm of the dead in search of his beloved wife, Eurydice, who had tragically died. As Orpheus made his way through the shadowy realm, it was Hecate who assisted him as a guide and protector.

Hecate's knowledge of the paths and passages of the Underworld allowed her to lead Orpheus safely through the treacherous terrain. She provided him with guidance and helped him navigate the realm of the dead, ensuring that he stayed on the correct path and avoided the dangers that lurked in the shadows.

Hecate's role as a guide between the living and the dead is further emphasised by her association with the torch, which symbolises illumination and guidance in dark places. In some versions of the myth, Hecate is depicted holding a torch to light Orpheus' way in the Underworld.

While this particular myth does not solely focus on Hecate's role as a guide between realms, it does highlight her assistance in navigating the realm of the dead and her ability to aid those who seek passage to or from the Underworld. Hecate's association with the liminal spaces, such as crossroads and thresholds, further reinforces her connection to the transition between life and death.

This myth illustrates Hecate's crucial role as a guide of souls and emphasises her ability to traverse the realms and provide assistance to those undertaking perilous journeys. In this context, she becomes not only a psychopomp but also a guardian and facilitator for individuals seeking passage into or out of the realm of the dead.

While the myth of Orpheus highlights Hecate's role as a guide of souls, it's important to note that she is not as prominently featured in this capacity as other deities like Hermes, who is often considered the primary psychopomp in Greek mythology. Nonetheless, Hecate's association with crossroads, boundaries, and transitions aligns her with the liminal spaces and moments that are significant in the journey of the soul.

Hecate's role as a guide of souls also extends beyond Greek mythology. In later mystical traditions and folk beliefs, particularly in the Hellenistic and Roman eras, Hecate was often invoked for her assistance in matters related to the afterlife and the spirit world. Her connection to witchcraft, magic, and the unseen realms made her a natural figure to seek guidance and protection from during funerary rites, deathbed rituals, and practices involving the spirits of the departed.

While Hecate's role as a guide to the underworld is not as extensively documented in mythology as some other deities, there are a few additional instances where her involvement in guiding souls can be found:

The Homeric Hymn to Demeter:

In this ancient Greek hymn, Hecate is mentioned as one of the deities who accompanied Demeter on her search for her daughter Persephone, who had been abducted by Hades. As they descended into the underworld, Hecate served as a guide, leading the way, and ensuring their safe passage through the realm of the dead.

The "Shield of Heracles" attributed to Hesiod:
This poem describes the hero Heracles' descent into the underworld. Hecate is mentioned as the one who provided him with the magical herbs needed to protect himself during his journey and return to the world of the living.

Sing, goddess, of the mighty shield of Heracles,
wrought by Hephaestus, the renowned craftsman,
that gleamed like the sun with its golden brilliance.
Upon it, the gods of Olympus were skilfully engraved,
and wondrous scenes adorned its radiant surface.
At the centre, Heracles himself stood strong and tall,
his lion-skin draped over his powerful shoulders,
and in his hands, he held his massive club.
Around him, fierce battles unfolded in vivid detail:
the clash of armies, the charge of chariots,
the piercing cries of warriors in combat.
On one side, the shield displayed a flourishing city,
with busy streets and bustling markets,
while on the other side, a peaceful countryside,
where farmers toiled and flocks grazed in tranquillity.
Amidst the scenes, gods and goddesses appeared,
watching over mortals with their divine gaze.
And there, at the shield's rim, stood Hecate,
the goddess of crossroads and magic,
a torch in one hand, a key in the other.
Her presence invoked mystery and power,
as she guarded the thresholds and guided souls.
Such was the shield of Heracles,
a symbol of his might and divine protection,
wielded in his heroic quests and epic battles,
a testament to the artistry of Hephaestus,
and a reflection of the gods' eternal presence.

Sing, goddess, of this magnificent shield,
and the hero who carried it to glory and fame.

The Orphic Hymns:

These hymns, part of the ancient Orphic tradition, invoke and praise various deities. The hymn to Hecate specifically describes her as the "torchbearer," guiding souls through the realms of Hades.

"Hail, Hecate, the mighty Queen of Night,
Who walks the shadowed realms in sacred might.
O lunar goddess, mistress of the crossroads,
You guide us through life's twists and turns, our souls you hold.
Goddess of magic, keeper of the key,
You hold the secrets of the ancient mystery.
With serpents twined in your hair so fair,
And torches blazing, your presence is rare.
Triple-formed Hecate, goddess divine,
We offer our reverence at your sacred shrine.
Grant us your wisdom, your protection, your grace,
As we walk the path with reverence and embrace.
Hecate, we call upon your name,
Guide us through darkness, bring us the flame.
In rituals and spells, we seek your aid,
With your power, our intentions are laid.
Mistress of the night, guardian of the dead,
Lead us through the underworld's sacred thread.
As we journey through realms unseen,
Your presence, Hecate, ever keen.
We honour you, Hecate, with love and praise,
In your triple form, we seek your ways.
Bless us, protect us, and show us the light,
Hecate, Queen of Night, shining bright."

May this hymn capture the essence of Hecate's power, guidance, and significance as you invoke her presence.

While these examples may not provide extensive narratives, they do reaffirm Hecate's role as a guide to the underworld in Greek mythology. It's important to note that Hecate's connections to the liminal spaces, her association with magic and crossroads, and her reputation as a guardian of boundaries and transitions, all contribute to her inherent ability to guide and facilitate journeys between realms, including the realm of the dead.

Myths and rituals related to Hecate's underworld connections.

Hecate's underworld connections are intertwined with various myths and rituals that highlight her role as a goddess who facilitates the journey between the realms of the living and the dead. Here are some examples of myths and rituals associated with Hecate's underworld connections:

In the myth of Persephone's abduction by Hades, Hecate is often depicted as an ally and companion to Persephone during her time in the underworld. Hecate aids Persephone in navigating her dual roles as the Queen of the Underworld and the Goddess of Spring. Hecate's presence emphasises her role in guiding souls and her connection to the realm of the dead.

When Demeter mourned the loss of her daughter Persephone, Hecate accompanied her on the journey to the underworld. As they traversed the realms of the dead, Hecate guided Demeter, helping her locate and retrieve Persephone from Hades' grasp. This myth underscores Hecate's role as a guide and protector in the realm of the dead.

The Deipnon and Hecate's Suppers:

In ancient Greek culture, Hecate was honoured through rituals known as the Deipnon and Hecate's Suppers. These practices were performed on the last day of the lunar month, known as the "dark moon" or the night of the new moon. Devotees would leave offerings, such as food, at crossroads or at the entrance of their homes to appease Hecate and seek her guidance in matters related to the spirit world and the deceased.

Necromancy and Divination:

Hecate was associated with practices of divination and necromancy, which involved communicating with the spirits of the dead. Individuals seeking insight or guidance from the underworld would invoke Hecate and perform rituals to gain access to the wisdom and knowledge of departed souls. These rituals often took place at night, in secluded places, and involved offerings and the use of special herbs and incantations.

Hecate's Keys and Torches:

In various depictions and symbolism, Hecate is portrayed holding keys and torches. These symbols represent her authority and power to unlock the gates of the underworld and illuminate the paths for souls seeking their way. The keys represent her control over access to the realm of the dead, while the torches symbolise her role as a guiding light for those embarking on their journey beyond the mortal realm.

These myths and rituals associated with Hecate's underworld connections highlight her role as a guide and mediator between the realms of the living and the dead. They demonstrate her ability to navigate the mysteries of the underworld, offer protection and guidance to souls, and grant access to the wisdom and insights of the deceased.

Chapter 7. Hecate in the Modern World.

Hecate's influence in contemporary spirituality and neopaganism is a fascinating aspect to explore. Here are some key points to consider when discussing Hecate's influence in the modern world:

Revival of Ancient Deities:

In the modern world, there has been a resurgence of interest in ancient mythologies and deities. Hecate, with her rich mythology and multifaceted symbolism, has captured the imagination of many individuals seeking to connect with the ancient wisdom and traditions. She has found a place in contemporary spirituality and neopaganism as a powerful and enigmatic goddess.

Goddess of Witchcraft and Magic:

Hecate's association with witchcraft, magic, and the occult has particularly resonated with modern practitioners. As a patroness of witchcraft, she is revered by witches, Wiccans, and other magical traditions. Hecate's energy is seen as potent for rituals, spell work, divination, and accessing the hidden realms of intuition and psychic abilities.

Archetype of the Wise Woman:

Hecate embodies the archetype of the wise woman, representing the aspects of feminine power, intuition, and wisdom. In modern spirituality, many women and men are drawn to Hecate as a symbol of empowerment, independence, and self-discovery. She is seen as a guide and mentor for those seeking to reclaim their personal power and connect with their authentic selves.

Crossroads and Life Transitions:

Hecate's association with crossroads and her role as a guide in decision-making and life transitions have resonated deeply with individuals navigating their own paths. In the modern world, people often seek Hecate's guidance when faced with important choices, major life transitions, or personal transformations. She is seen as a source of strength and wisdom during times of uncertainty and change.

Lunar Phases and Goddess of the Moon:

Hecate's connection to lunar phases and her role as a lunar goddess have also found relevance in contemporary spirituality. Many practitioners honour and work with Hecate during specific lunar phases, such as the full moon or the dark moon. They seek to align themselves with the natural cycles of the moon, tapping into Hecate's transformative energies and embracing the symbolism of the lunar journey.

Rituals and Devotion:

Modern followers of Hecate often engage in rituals, devotional practices, and offerings to honour and connect with her. These may include lighting candles, reciting prayers, or invocations, creating altars, and performing specific rituals associated with Hecate. These practices serve as ways to establish a personal relationship with the goddess and seek her guidance, protection, and blessings.

In Wiccan belief systems, Hecate is often revered as a powerful goddess associated with witchcraft, magic, and the moon. She is seen as a guardian and guide, offering her wisdom and protection to witches and practitioners of the Craft. Wiccans may invoke Hecate's presence during rituals, spells, and ceremonies, seeking her assistance in matters of divination, spellcasting, and personal transformation.

Hecate's association with the moon is especially relevant in Wiccan lunar rituals. Wiccans commonly celebrate the phases of the moon, such as the full moon or new moon, and during these lunar rituals, they may call upon Hecate's energy and symbolism to enhance their magical workings and connect with the intuitive and transformative powers of the lunar cycle.

Wiccans who work with Hecate may create dedicated altars or shrines to honour her, featuring candles, symbols, and offerings that represent her attributes and energies. They may also incorporate

Hecate-specific rituals or invocations into their practice, drawing upon her qualities of protection, guidance, and connection to the liminal spaces between realms.

Modern interpretations and worship of Hecate

Modern interpretations and worship of Hecate have evolved in various ways, reflecting the diverse beliefs and practices of contemporary followers. Here are some key aspects to consider when discussing modern interpretations and worship of Hecate:

Eclectic Spirituality:

Hecate's worship and devotion in modern times often embrace eclectic spiritual practices. Individuals may incorporate elements from various traditions, such as Wicca, witchcraft, Hellenic reconstructionism, and other pagan paths. This eclecticism allows for a personalised approach to honouring Hecate while incorporating contemporary beliefs and rituals.

Goddess of Transformation:

In modern interpretations, Hecate is often seen as a goddess of transformation and personal growth. Followers may invoke her energy to assist in inner healing, shadow work, and navigating life's challenges. Hecate's association with crossroads and her role as a guide in transitions make her a symbol of personal empowerment and transformation.

Magic and Witchcraft:

Hecate is strongly associated with magic and witchcraft in modern interpretations. Many practitioners of magic and witchcraft seek her guidance, blessings, and assistance in spell work, divination, and intuitive practices. Rituals and offerings dedicated to Hecate may involve spellcasting, creating talismans, or engaging in rituals that tap into her transformative and mystical energies.

Psychopomp and Ancestral Connections:

In modern interpretations and worship of Hecate, one significant aspect that holds great fascination is her role as a psychopomp, a guide of souls. Drawing from her association with the underworld and her ability to traverse different realms, Hecate is seen as a powerful mediator between the living and the dead.

As a psychopomp, Hecate is believed to assist and accompany souls in their journey from the earthly realm to the realm of the afterlife. She ensures safe passage and guides them through the transitional spaces, helping them navigate the intricate paths of the underworld. In this capacity, Hecate offers comfort, protection, and guidance to those who have departed from this world.

Her connection to the realm of the dead also extends to ancestral connections. Many modern practitioners and worshipers of Hecate seek her assistance in communicating with their ancestors and honouring their lineage. Through rituals, offerings, and meditation, individuals establish a connection with their ancestral spirits and seek their wisdom, guidance, and blessings.

Hecate's association with the underworld and her role as a psychopomp resonates deeply with those who seek to honour their ancestors and maintain a spiritual connection with them. She is believed to facilitate communication and provide a link between the realms, enabling individuals to receive messages, guidance, and support from their ancestral lineage.

In contemporary practices, individuals often incorporate elements of ancestral veneration into their rituals dedicated to Hecate. Offerings such as food, drink, and symbolic items are presented to both Hecate and the honoured ancestors as a gesture of respect and remembrance. Prayers, invocations, and meditations are employed to establish a sacred connection and seek the wisdom and blessings of both Hecate and the ancestral spirits.

Lunar Goddess and Moon Magic:

Hecate's connection to lunar phases and the moon has continued to inspire modern interpretations. Many followers align their rituals and devotional practices with specific lunar phases, honouring Hecate's association with the moon's cycles. Moon rituals, meditation, and spell work may be performed to harness the energies of the different lunar phases and connect with Hecate's transformative power.

Community and Online Platforms:

Modern worship of Hecate often thrives within online communities and social media platforms. These spaces provide opportunities for practitioners to share knowledge, experiences, and rituals dedicated to Hecate. Online groups and forums foster connections among individuals who resonate with Hecate's energy, allowing for the exchange of ideas, rituals, and personal insights.

Personal Devotion and Offerings:

Modern worship of Hecate emphasises personal devotion and offerings. Followers may create altars dedicated to Hecate, adorned with symbols, images, candles, and offerings such as herbs, crystals, or food items associated with her. Regular devotional practices, such as prayers, invocations, and meditation, help establish and strengthen the relationship between the devotee and Hecate.

Here are some examples of herbs, crystals, flowers, and food that can be used as personal devotion offerings to Hecate:

Herbs:

1. Mug wort: Mug wort is associated with Hecate and is believed to enhance psychic abilities and spiritual connection.

2. Lavender: Lavender is known for its calming and purifying properties, making it a suitable offering for Hecate's presence.

3. Rosemary: Rosemary is often used in rituals for protection and clarity, making it a fitting herb to honour Hecate's association with magic and guidance.

4. Yarrow: Yarrow is considered a powerful herb in divination and is associated with Hecate's ability to reveal hidden knowledge.

Crystals:

1. Obsidian: Obsidian is a protective stone that can be offered to Hecate to enhance spiritual insight and transformation.

2. Moonstone: Moonstone resonates with the lunar energies associated with Hecate and can aid in enhancing intuition and divination.

3. Labradorite: Labradorite is believed to enhance psychic abilities and spiritual connection, making it a suitable offering to Hecate.

4. Black Tourmaline: Black Tourmaline is a grounding and protective stone that can be used to create a safe and sacred space for Hecate's energy.

Flowers:

1. Hellebore: Hellebore, also known as the Christmas, rose, is associated with Hecate, and is often used as an offering in rituals and ceremonies.

2. Night-blooming flowers: Flowers that bloom at night, such as moonflowers or evening primroses, are often associated with Hecate's nocturnal nature and can be offered to honour her.

3. Lavender: Lavender flowers not only have a pleasant scent but also symbolise serenity and protection, making them a suitable offering to Hecate.

4. Marigold: Marigolds are associated with the cycles of life and death, making them a meaningful offering to Hecate as a goddess of liminal spaces and transitions.

Food and Libations:

1. Honey: Honey is a sweet offering that is often associated with Hecate. It symbolises abundance, fertility, and the sweetness of life.

2. Garlic: Garlic is believed to have protective qualities and can be offered to Hecate as a symbol of warding off negative energies and evil spirits.

3. Pomegranate: The pomegranate is associated with the underworld and represents fertility and abundance. It is a significant offering in rituals honouring Hecate's connection to the realms of life and death.

4. Wine or herbal tea: Offerings of wine or herbal tea can be made to Hecate as libations, symbolising communion, and the sharing of energy.

When making offerings to Hecate, it is important to do so with sincerity, respect, and gratitude. Follow your intuition and choose items that resonate with your personal connection to Hecate and your intention for the offering.

It is important to note that modern interpretations and worship of Hecate can vary widely among individuals and communities. Each practitioner may have their own unique approach and personal connection with the goddess, blending ancient traditions with contemporary beliefs and practices. The diverse interpretations and worship of Hecate reflect the vibrant and evolving nature of modern spirituality.

Hecate in Comparative Mythology and Religions

Exploring parallels and connections between Hecate and deities from other mythological traditions can reveal intriguing similarities and shared attributes. Here are some examples of connections and parallels that can be explored:

Triple Goddesses:

Hecate's triple form as Maiden, Mother, and Crone finds parallels in other mythological traditions. For instance, in Celtic mythology, the goddess Brigid embodies similar triple aspects as a goddess of poetry, healing, and smithcraft. In Hinduism, the goddess Durga represents the triple aspects of divine femininity as Kali, Lakshmi, and Saraswati. These connections highlight the archetypal presence of the Triple Goddess across different cultures.

Underworld Deities:

Hecate's association with the realm of the dead and her role as a psychopomp can be paralleled with other underworld deities. In the ancient Egyptian tradition, the goddess Isis shares similarities as a guide of souls and a protective figure. In Norse mythology, the goddess Hel rules over the realm of the dead. These connections emphasise the cross-cultural presence of deities associated with the afterlife and transitions between realms.

Lunar Goddesses:

Hecate's connection to lunar phases and her role as a lunar goddess can be compared to deities from other mythologies linked to the moon. In the Norse tradition, the goddess Frigg has lunar associations, while in Hinduism, the goddess Chandra represents the moon. These parallels illustrate the universal recognition of the moon as a symbol of feminine power and its association with various goddess figures.

Witchcraft and Magic:

Hecate's association with witchcraft, sorcery, and magic can be seen in parallel with deities and figures from other mythologies linked to similar practices. In Norse mythology, the goddess Freya is associated with magic, divination, and seidr. In Slavic folklore, the witch Baba Yaga embodies similar qualities as a wise, mysterious figure with magical abilities. These connections highlight the presence of powerful magical figures across different cultural narratives.

Crossroad Guardians:

Hecate's role as the guardian of crossroads can find parallels in other mythological traditions. In Roman mythology, the god Janus presides over crossroads, gateways, and transitions. In Yoruba mythology, the orisha Eshu/Elegba is associated with crossroads and serves as a messenger and intermediary. These connections emphasise the recognition of crossroads as liminal spaces that require guidance and protection.

Hecate's influence on later goddesses and figures in different cultures

Hecate's influence can be seen in later goddesses and figures within various cultures, demonstrating the enduring impact of her archetypal qualities. Here are some examples of Hecate's influence on later goddesses and figures:

Diana/Artemis (Roman/Greek):

Hecate's association with the moon, crossroads, and her role as a huntress influenced the depiction of Diana in Roman mythology and Artemis in Greek mythology. Like Hecate, Diana/Artemis is associated with the wilderness, the moon, and is often depicted with a bow and arrow. They share the attributes of independence, wildness, and protective qualities.

Persephone (Greek):

Hecate's connection to the underworld and her role as a guide of souls influenced the myth of Persephone, who became the queen of the underworld after being abducted by Hades. Hecate is sometimes depicted alongside Persephone during her descent and return from the underworld, emphasising their intertwined roles in the realm of the dead.

Cerridwen (Celtic):

Hecate's association with magic and her role as a wise crone influenced the figure of Cerridwen in Celtic mythology. Cerridwen is a powerful enchantress and keeper of wisdom and transformation. Like Hecate, she is often associated with cauldrons, magic, and the mysteries of the Otherworld.

Isis (Egyptian):

Hecate's role as a guardian, protector, and guide of souls influenced the goddess Isis in ancient Egyptian mythology. Isis is often depicted with wings, representing her protective nature and ability to guide souls in the afterlife. Both Hecate and Isis share attributes related to the liminal spaces between life and death and their roles as psychopomps.

Baba Yaga (Slavic folklore):

Hecate's association with witchcraft, sorcery, and her role as a wise crone influenced the figure of Baba Yaga in Slavic folklore. Baba Yaga is depicted as a powerful and enigmatic witch, often living in a house that stands on chicken legs. Like Hecate, she possesses wisdom, magical abilities, and guards the boundaries between the mundane and supernatural realms.

These examples demonstrate how Hecate's characteristics and symbolism have influenced the portrayal of later goddesses and figures across different cultures. Hecate's archetypal presence and her diverse roles as a lunar goddess, guide of souls, wise crone, and guardian of crossroads have resonated with people and have been reimagined and integrated into various mythologies and folklore over time.

Hecate as a Symbol of Feminine Power and Wisdom

Goddess of Wisdom

Hecate is associated with wisdom, particularly the type of wisdom that comes from intuition, deep knowing, and understanding the mysteries of the universe. She embodies the wisdom gained through experience and the ability to navigate complex situations. As the goddess of crossroads, she represents the wisdom of making choices and taking decisive actions. Hecate is often depicted as a wise crone, symbolising the accumulated knowledge and insight that comes with age and experience.

Goddess of Magic:

Hecate's association with magic is prominent in her mythology. She is revered as a powerful sorceress and enchantress, capable of wielding transformative and mystical energies. Hecate is considered the patroness of witchcraft, offering guidance and assistance to those who practice magical arts. Her connection to the unseen realms and her role as a guide of souls further reinforces her association with magical practices, divination, and accessing hidden knowledge.

Feminine Strength:

Hecate embodies the essence of feminine strength and empowerment. She represents the power and resilience of women and the inherent strength found within femininity. Hecate is often depicted as independent, assertive, and self-reliant. She is a symbol of female empowerment and the ability to embrace one's own personal power. Hecate's association with the moon, a symbol of the feminine, further reinforces her connection to feminine strength and intuition.

Together, Hecate's roles as a goddess of wisdom, magic, and feminine strength form a powerful archetype that resonates with many individuals seeking guidance, empowerment, and connection to their inner selves. She encourages the exploration of intuitive wisdom, the pursuit of magical practices, and the embrace of one's own inner strength. Hecate's influence extends beyond ancient mythology, as she continues to inspire and guide those who seek wisdom, magic, and the embodiment of feminine strength in their lives.

Feminist interpretations and reclaiming of Hecate's archetype.

Feminist interpretations and the reclaiming of Hecate's archetype have become significant aspects of contemporary spiritual and cultural movements. Here are some points to consider when discussing feminist interpretations and the reclaiming of Hecate's archetype:

Embracing the Dark Feminine:

Hecate is often associated with the dark or shadow aspects of femininity. Feminist interpretations seek to reclaim and celebrate these aspects, challenging the traditional dichotomy of light and dark ascribed to women. By embracing Hecate's archetype, feminists aim to reclaim and honour the strength, wisdom, and power that can be found in the shadow aspects of femininity.

Autonomy and Sovereignty:

Hecate's independence and autonomy are celebrated in feminist interpretations. She represents a powerful figure who makes her own choices and follows her own path, unaffected by societal expectations or patriarchal norms. Feminists view Hecate as a symbol of female agency and sovereignty, inspiring women to embrace their own autonomy and assert their individuality.

Magic and Intuition:

Feminist interpretations of Hecate emphasise her association with magic and intuition. They encourage women to reclaim and embrace their own intuitive powers and innate connection to the mysteries of the universe. Hecate's archetype is seen as a source of inspiration for reclaiming and celebrating the power of feminine intuition, psychic abilities, and magical practices.

Reclaiming the Crone:

Hecate's depiction as a wise crone is particularly significant in feminist interpretations. The figure of the crone challenges societal expectations around youth and beauty, offering an alternative narrative that values wisdom, experience, and the aging process. Feminists seek to reclaim and honour the wisdom and power inherent in the stage of life often associated with the crone, viewing it as a time of transformation, self-discovery, and empowerment.

Intersectionality and Inclusivity:

Feminist interpretations of Hecate aim to be inclusive and intersectional, recognising that women's experiences and identities are diverse. They acknowledge the importance of inclusivity by embracing Hecate's archetype as a symbol of empowerment for women of all backgrounds, including those who identify as LGBTQ+, BIPOC (Black, Indigenous, and People of Colour), and other marginalised groups.

By reclaiming Hecate's archetype through feminist interpretations, individuals and communities seek to challenge traditional gender roles, empower women, celebrate diverse forms of femininity, and create spaces where all women can embrace their unique strengths and identities. These interpretations provide a lens through which Hecate's symbolism can be seen as a source of inspiration and empowerment for feminist movements.

Hecate's relevance in empowering women and celebrating the divine feminine.

Hecate holds great relevance in empowering women and celebrating the divine feminine. Here are some key points to consider:

Hecate's archetype and symbolism provide inspiration for women to reclaim their power, autonomy, and agency. By embodying the qualities associated with Hecate, women can draw upon her strength, wisdom, and magical prowess to assert themselves in various aspects of life. Hecate serves as a powerful role model for women, encouraging them to embrace their own inner strength and navigate life's challenges with confidence.

Hecate represents the divine feminine in all its forms, celebrating the unique qualities and contributions of women. She embodies the interconnectedness of femininity, intuition, wisdom, and nurturing energies. By recognising and honouring the divine feminine within themselves and others, individuals can foster a greater appreciation for the diverse expressions of femininity and the valuable roles women play in society.

Hecate's association with magic, witchcraft, and intuition encourages women to trust their inner knowing and tap into their psychic abilities. She reminds women of the power of intuition as a guiding force in decision-making, personal growth, and spiritual exploration. By embracing their innate intuitive gifts, women can enhance their self-awareness, deepen their connection to the spiritual realm, and navigate life's complexities with greater clarity.

Hecate's triple aspect as Maiden, Mother, and Crone highlights the significance of embracing the full life cycle and the different stages of womanhood. By recognising and honouring the transformative journey from youth to maturity, women can find empowerment and self-acceptance at every stage. Hecate's representation of the wise crone encourages women to embrace their accumulated wisdom, life experiences, and the richness that comes with age.

Hecate's role as a guardian of crossroads and liminal spaces encourages unity and collaboration among women. She symbolises the power of sisterhood and collective support. By fostering a sense of community and solidarity, women can uplift and empower one another, creating spaces for mutual growth, shared wisdom, and collective empowerment.

Hecate's relevance in empowering women and celebrating the divine feminine lies in her embodiment of strength, wisdom, intuition, and the nurturing aspects of femininity. By embracing her archetype and exploring her symbolism, individuals can tap into these qualities to foster personal empowerment, spiritual growth, and a greater appreciation for the diverse expressions of the divine feminine. Hecate's influence continues to inspire women to embrace their inherent power and contribute to a world that celebrates and uplifts the strengths and contributions of all women.

Chapter 8: Invocation of Hecate Today

In contemporary Pagan, Wiccan and Witchcraft practices, Hecate continues to be revered and invoked as a powerful deity. Her ancient associations with magic, witchcraft, crossroads, and the mysteries of the night make her a compelling figure for modern practitioners. This chapter explores the pagan invocation of Hecate in present-day rituals, offering insights into how individuals connect with her energy and seek her guidance in their spiritual practices.

The Relevance of Hecate in Modern Practices:

In modern Paganism, Hecate continues to hold great significance and remains a beloved and revered goddess among practitioners. Her multifaceted nature and associations with magic, witchcraft, crossroads, and liminal spaces make her an appealing and powerful figure for those on a Pagan path.

Hecate's strong association with witchcraft resonates deeply with modern Wiccan and Witchcraft traditions. She is seen as a patroness of practitioners, guiding them in their magical workings and offering protection and wisdom on their spiritual journey.

Hecate's role as a guide between realms, particularly as a psychopomp who escorts souls to the afterlife, remains significant in modern Pagan beliefs. Many Pagans invoke Hecate's assistance in journeying between the worlds, seeking guidance, and connecting with ancestral spirits.

Hecate embodies the transformative powers of magic and personal growth. Modern Pagans turn to her for assistance in navigating life's transitions, embracing change, and embracing their own inner power. She symbolises the transformative journey from darkness to light, ignorance to wisdom, and fear to empowerment.

The concept of crossroads as symbolic places of choice and transition holds relevance in modern Paganism. Hecate's association with crossroads speaks to the importance of making conscious decisions and embracing the opportunities and challenges that come with them. Pagans often seek Hecate's guidance when faced with significant life choices or when seeking direction on their spiritual path.

Hecate's connection to the moon and its phases aligns with the cyclical nature of life and the spiritual significance of lunar energy in modern Paganism. Many Pagans honour Hecate during specific lunar phases, perform rituals, and invoke her guidance for personal and magical workings.

Hecate's portrayal as a powerful, independent goddess represents the divine feminine and serves as a symbol of empowerment for modern Pagans, especially women. Her ability to embrace the shadow, access deep wisdom, and stand strong in her sovereignty inspires individuals to embrace their own strength, intuition, and magical potential.

In modern Paganism, the worship and invocation of Hecate continue to evolve, with practitioners adapting her symbols, rituals, and imagery to suit their individual spiritual practices. Whether through personal devotion, group ceremonies, spell work, or the exploration of her mythology, Hecate remains a relevant and revered figure in modern Paganism, offering guidance, protection, and empowerment to those who seek her wisdom and embrace her presence.

Establishing a Connection with Hecate:

Before invoking Hecate, it is important to establish a personal connection with her. Connecting with Hecate can be a deeply personal and transformative experience. Whether you are a beginner or an experienced practitioner, here are some ways to foster a meaningful connection with Hecate:

- Start by immersing yourself in the myths, stories, and symbols associated with Hecate. Learn about her roles, attributes, and the historical and cultural contexts in which she was revered. This knowledge will deepen your understanding and appreciation of her significance.

- Set aside quiet time for meditation and reflection. Create a sacred space where you can sit or lie comfortably. Close your eyes, breathe deeply, and visualise Hecate's presence. Invite her into your meditation and allow her energy to envelop you. Use this time to listen, receive guidance, and deepen your connection.

- Show your reverence and dedication to Hecate by offering her gifts. These can include herbs, crystals, flowers, incense, or symbolic items associated with her. Offerings can also include acts of service, such as volunteering or supporting causes that align with her values. Regularly express your devotion and gratitude to deepen the bond.

- Incorporate Hecate into your ritual and spell work practices. Design rituals specifically goddicated to her, invoking her presence, and seeking her guidance. Craft spells aligned with her areas of influence, such as protection, transformation, or divination. Use Hecate's symbols and imagery to enhance the energy and intention of your magical workings.

- As Hecate is closely associated with crossroads, consider incorporating crossroads work into your practice. Physically visit a crossroads and make offerings, meditate, or seek guidance. Metaphorically, view crossroads as opportunities for personal growth and decision-making, seeking Hecate's wisdom and guidance when faced with important choices.

- Honour Hecate's connection to the moon by incorporating lunar rituals into your practice. Perform ceremonies or spells during specific lunar phases, such as the new moon or full moon, to harness the energy of the moon and connect with Hecate's power. Use moon symbolism, such as silver candles or lunar correspondences, to amplify the ritual's intention.

- Ultimately, connecting with Hecate is a deeply personal experience. Allow yourself to develop your own unique relationship with her. Listen to your intuition, follow the guidance that resonates with you, and trust the messages and signs that come your way. Cultivate an open heart and mind, inviting Hecate to walk beside you on your spiritual journey.

Building a connection with Hecate takes time and dedication. Be patient and persistent in your efforts, and trust that she will respond in her own way and time. Stay open to the lessons and blessings she brings and allow her energy to guide and empower you on your spiritual path.

Ritual Practices for Invoking Hecate:

Hecate is strongly associated with various aspects of magic, witchcraft, and liminal spaces. Incorporating these associations into your magical practices can deepen your connection with her and enhance the potency of your spell work. Here are some ways to honour and incorporate Hecate's associations:

Spell work and Rituals: - Hecate is known as the goddess of magic and witchcraft. When performing spells or rituals, invoke Hecate's presence by calling upon her name and asking for her guidance and assistance. Focus on spells and rituals related to her areas of influence, such as protection, transformation, banishing, and divination. Incorporate her symbols, such as keys, torches, or the triple goddess symbol, into your spell work to amplify her energy.

Divination - Hecate is associated with divination and prophecy. Connect with her energy by using divination tools like tarot cards, runes, or scrying mirrors. Before beginning your divination practice, invite Hecate to join you and provide insights and guidance. Trust your intuition and pay attention to the messages and symbols that come through during your divination sessions, as they may carry Hecate's wisdom.

Herbalism: - Hecate is often associated with herbs and their magical properties. Explore herbalism by incorporating Hecate-associated plants into your practice. Some herbs associated with Hecate include mug wort, lavender, mandrake, belladonna, and yarrow. Use these herbs in spell jars, charm bags, or herbal teas to harness their magical properties and invite Hecate's blessings. Remember to research the properties and potential risks of each herb before use.

Liminal Spaces - Hecate is the goddess of crossroads and liminal spaces. To honour this aspect, seek out and visit physical crossroads, paying your respects to Hecate by leaving offerings or performing rituals. Additionally, you can create your own symbolic crossroads using stones, crystals, or even drawn symbols on the ground. Use these crossroads as focal points for spell work or as places of meditation and reflection, inviting Hecate's presence and guidance.

Ritual Tools and Symbols - Incorporate Hecate's symbols and ritual tools into your practice. Use keys, torches, knives, or besoms (brooms) as representations of her energy. Place these items on your altar or use them during rituals and spell work to invoke her presence and channel her power. Consider crafting your own ritual tools or sacred objects dedicated to Hecate to deepen your connection.

Offerings - Pay homage to Hecate by making offerings that align with her associations. Offerings can include wine, honey, garlic, eggs, pomegranates, or dark chocolate. These offerings can be placed on your altar or at crossroads as a gesture of gratitude and respect. Remember to dispose of offerings responsibly after the ritual, following your ethical guidelines and respecting the environment.

Moon Magic - Hecate's connection to the moon makes lunar magic a powerful way to honour her. Work with the phases of the moon, especially the new moon and full moon, to align with Hecate's energy. Perform rituals, spells, or meditation during these lunar phases to harness the transformative and illuminating qualities associated with Hecate and the moon.

Seeking Guidance and Wisdom:

Connecting with Hecate goes beyond simply invoking her presence. To deepen your bond and receive guidance from her, it is important to open yourself to her wisdom and insights. Here are some methods practitioners can use to seek guidance from Hecate during invocations:

Meditation - Meditation is a powerful practice for quieting the mind, centring yourself, and opening up to spiritual guidance. Begin by creating a sacred space for your meditation practice. Light candles or torches in honour of Hecate and set the intention to receive her guidance. You can use guided meditations specifically designed to connect with Hecate or simply sit in stillness and focus on her energy.

During your meditation, visualise yourself in a crossroads or liminal space, inviting Hecate to join you. Allow your mind to become receptive and open to any messages, images, or sensations that arise. Be patient and trust that Hecate will communicate with you in her own way, whether through symbols, insights, or intuitive thoughts. Take note of any guidance received and incorporate it into your spiritual practice or daily life.

Scrying - Scrying is a divinatory practice that involves gazing into a reflective surface, such as a mirror, a crystal ball, or a bowl of water, to receive spiritual messages and insights. To scry with Hecate's guidance, create a sacred space and set up your scrying tool of choice. Focus your attention on Hecate's energy and invite her to reveal messages through the scrying medium.

As you gaze into the reflective surface, allow your mind to relax and become receptive. Be open to any images, symbols, or impressions that come through. Trust your intuition and let the messages unfold naturally. Remember that scrying is a personal and intuitive practice, so the interpretations of the messages will be unique to you. Take your time and practice regularly to deepen your connection with Hecate through scrying.

Dreamwork - Hecate is associated with dreams and the realm of the unconscious. Before going to sleep, set the intention to connect with Hecate in your dreams and seek her guidance. Keep a dream journal by your bed to record any dreams or insights upon waking.

To enhance your dreamwork with Hecate, create a dream altar or space dedicated to her. Place symbols of Hecate, such as keys or torches, near your bed or on your nightstand. Before sleep, spend a few moments in meditation, inviting Hecate to enter your dreams and provide guidance. Upon waking, reflect on your dreams and look for any recurring symbols or themes that may carry Hecate's messages. Consider working with a dream journal or seeking guidance from experienced dream interpreters to gain deeper insights into Hecate's wisdom as revealed in your dreams.

Seeking guidance and wisdom from Hecate requires patience, trust, and a willingness to be open to her messages. Practice these methods regularly and cultivate a respectful and reverent relationship with her. As you deepen your connection, you may find that Hecate's guidance becomes an invaluable source of insight and spiritual growth in your life.

Integration into Daily Life:

Honouring Hecate's presence and teachings in your daily life is a powerful way to deepen your connection with her and embody her wisdom. Here are some ways practitioners can integrate Hecate into their everyday actions and decisions:

Awareness and Mindfulness - Cultivate a sense of awareness and mindfulness in your daily life. Pay attention to the liminal spaces and crossroads you encounter both physically and metaphorically. Recognise that life is full of choices, transitions, and opportunities for growth. By being present and mindful, you can actively engage with these moments and make conscious decisions aligned with Hecate's energy.

Reflection and Journaling - Set aside time for reflection and journaling to explore your thoughts, emotions, and experiences. Consider the lessons and teachings that Hecate has imparted to you during your invocations and rituals. Write down any insights, synchronicities, or messages you have received. Use your journal as a tool for self-discovery and personal growth, allowing Hecate's presence to guide your introspection and reflection.

Regular Practices - Maintain a regular spiritual practice that includes meditation, prayer, or devotion to Hecate. Set aside dedicated time each day or week to connect with her, express gratitude, and seek her guidance. Meditate on her symbols, chant her invocations, or recite prayers specific to her. By consistently engaging in these practices, you create a sacred space for Hecate within your life, fostering a deeper connection and alignment with her energy.

Acts of Service - Embody Hecate's teachings by performing acts of service to others and the world around you. Offer your time, skills, or resources to those in need or to causes that resonate with Hecate's values. This could involve volunteering, participating in community projects, or advocating for social and environmental justice. By serving others, you align yourself with Hecate's compassionate and nurturing aspects, actively contributing to the betterment of the world.

Rituals in Daily Life - Infuse your everyday actions and routines with ritualistic intention. Consider how you can incorporate Hecate's energy into your daily activities, such as cooking meals with intention and gratitude, creating altars or sacred spaces in your home, or incorporating Hecate's symbols and offerings into your work or creative endeavours. By infusing your daily life with ritual, you invite Hecate's presence into the mundane, finding meaning and connection in the simplest of tasks.

Integrating Hecate into daily life is an ongoing practice that requires dedication and intention. It is through consistent engagement and embodiment of her teachings that her presence becomes a guiding force in your decisions and actions. By weaving her energy into your daily experiences, you create a harmonious and transformative relationship with Hecate that extends beyond the boundaries of specific rituals or invocations.

Understanding Hecate's Energy:

Before invoking Hecate, it is essential to develop an understanding of her archetypal qualities, her associations with magic, and her role as a guide and guardian. This understanding will help practitioners establish a more meaningful connection with Hecate during invocations.

Hecate embodies a multifaceted archetypal energy that encompasses various aspects of the divine feminine. She is often associated with the Triple Goddess, representing the stages of maiden, mother, and crone. As the goddess of crossroads and liminal spaces, she symbolises transitions, choices, and the potential for growth and transformation. Additionally, Hecate is known as a guardian, protector, and guide who holds deep wisdom and insight. Understanding these archetypal qualities allows practitioners to tap into the full spectrum of Hecate's energy.

Hecate is widely regarded as the goddess of magic, witchcraft, and the occult. She possesses a deep understanding of the mystical arts and is revered as a powerful source of magical knowledge and transformation. As practitioners seek to connect with Hecate, it is important to acknowledge and honour her associations with magic. This can involve studying magical traditions, working with spells and rituals that align with her energy, and exploring divination and other mystical practices. By immersing oneself in Hecate's magical realms, practitioners can deepen their connection with her energy and tap into her transformative power.

Hecate serves as a guide and guardian, leading individuals through the realms of the physical and the spiritual. She is known as a psychopomp, assisting souls in their journey from the living to the realm of the dead. In invoking Hecate, practitioners can seek her guidance and wisdom to navigate their own personal journeys. Whether it is making important decisions, navigating life's crossroads, or seeking spiritual insight, Hecate's energy can provide clarity and support. Recognising her role as a guide and guardian allows practitioners to establish a deep trust in her guidance and embrace her presence as a constant companion.

Establishing a meaningful connection with Hecate requires an understanding and appreciation of her archetypal qualities, her associations with magic, and her role as a guide and guardian. By delving into these aspects, practitioners can cultivate a deeper resonance with her energy, allowing for more profound and transformative invocations. Through this understanding, practitioners can forge a powerful connection with Hecate and invite her wisdom and guidance into their lives.

Connection to the Underworld:

Hecate's role as a guide and guardian of the underworld is another vital aspect of her energy. As the goddess who traverses between the realms of the living and the dead, she possesses profound knowledge of the mysteries of life, death, and rebirth. Her connection to the underworld signifies her ability to assist in shadow work, inner transformation, and connecting with ancestral wisdom. Invoking Hecate's energy can help practitioners navigate personal depths, face fears, and access hidden aspects of themselves.

Guide and Guardian:

Hecate is revered as a guide and guardian, particularly at crossroads. She is often depicted holding torches, illuminating the path, and providing guidance to those who seek her assistance. Invoking Hecate's energy can help practitioners make decisions, navigate transitions, and find direction in their lives. As a guardian, she offers protection, particularly in liminal spaces and during rites of passage. Understanding Hecate's role as a guide and guardian allows practitioners to approach invocations with a sense of reverence and trust.

By delving into Hecate's archetypal qualities, associations with witchcraft and magic, connection to the underworld, and role as a guide and guardian, practitioners can develop a profound understanding of her energy. This understanding lays the foundation for establishing a genuine and meaningful connection during invocations. It enables practitioners to align with Hecate's transformative powers, seek her guidance, and harness her energy in their spiritual practices.

Setting Sacred Space:

Creating a sacred space is an essential step in invoking Hecate's presence and establishing a conducive environment for spiritual connection. This section explores various techniques for setting up a sacred space that aligns with Hecate's energy. It discusses the preparation of an altar, the selection of appropriate symbols, and the incorporation of relevant items that represent Hecate's essence. It also explores the significance of invoking Hecate at crossroads or at night to tap into her liminal nature.

Choosing the Sacred Space:

Selecting an appropriate location for your sacred space is crucial. It can be a dedicated room, a secluded corner of your home, or even an outdoor area if feasible. Consider a space where you can maintain privacy and where you feel comfortable and connected to the energies of Hecate.

Preparing the Altar:

The altar serves as a focal point for invoking Hecate's presence. Clear the space and cleanse it energetically using methods such as smudging, sacred herbs, or visualisation. Arrange the altar in a way that feels meaningful to you, keeping in mind Hecate's associations. Consider incorporating elements such as candles, herbs, crystals, and symbolic representations of keys, torches, snakes, or the moon.

Selecting Symbols:

Choose symbols that resonate with Hecate's energy to enhance the sacred space. Keys symbolise unlocking hidden knowledge and opening doors to new possibilities. Torches represent illumination and guidance. Snakes symbolise transformation and the shedding of old patterns. The moon, in its various phases, reflects Hecate's association with lunar cycles and mysteries. Incorporating these symbols helps to create a visual representation of Hecate's essence.

Relevant Items and Offerings:

Incorporate items and offerings that honour Hecate's energy and significance. This could include specific herbs associated with her, such as mug wort, lavender, or mandrake. Offerings like honey, pomegranates, or wine can be placed on the altar as symbols of abundance and connection to the underworld. Consider including a small bowl of water to represent the liminal spaces Hecate traverses.

Invoking Hecate at Crossroads or at Night:

To further align with Hecate's liminal nature, consider invoking her at crossroads or during night-time rituals. Crossroads are symbolically significant as places where paths intersect and choices are made. By invoking Hecate at crossroads, practitioners seek her guidance and wisdom in navigating life's choices and transitions. The night-time, particularly during the dark moon or when the moon is in its waning phase, amplifies Hecate's associations with the mysteries of the night, magic, and the unseen realms.

Creating a sacred space that incorporates symbols, items, and offerings aligned with Hecate's energy helps to establish a connection with her during invocations. By invoking Hecate at crossroads or during the night-time, practitioners tap into her liminal nature and enhance the potency of their rituals. It is important to personalise and adapt these techniques based on your own spiritual beliefs and practices, allowing for a deeply meaningful and authentic connection with Hecate.

Ritual Invocations:

This section provides guidance on crafting invocations specific to Hecate. It explores different poetic and prose styles that can be used to invoke her presence, honour her attributes, and seek her guidance. It also encourages personalisation and adaptation of invocations to suit individual spiritual practices and intentions.

Ritual Invocations:

Crafting invocations specific to Hecate is a powerful way to call upon her presence, honour her attributes, and seek her guidance. This section provides guidance on creating invocations that resonate with Hecate's energy. It explores different poetic and prose styles that can be used to invoke her presence and convey heartfelt intentions. It also encourages personalisation and adaptation of invocations to suit individual spiritual practices and intentions.

Connecting with Hecate's Attributes:

Before crafting an invocation, take time to reflect on Hecate's attributes and the qualities you wish to invoke. Consider her associations with magic, wisdom, empowerment, transformation, and guidance. Reflect on how these attributes align with your intentions and the specific assistance you seek from Hecate. This reflection will help infuse your invocation with sincerity and personal meaning.

Poetic Styles:

Poetry is a powerful medium for invoking Hecate's presence. Consider exploring different poetic styles such as free verse, sonnets, or haikus to convey your intentions. Use vivid imagery, metaphors, and symbolism to evoke the essence of Hecate. Incorporate rhythmic patterns or repetition to create a sense of ritualistic flow. Experiment with the use of alliteration, assonance, or other literary devices to enhance the potency of your invocation.

Prose Styles:

Prose invocations offer a more straightforward and narrative approach to calling upon Hecate. Write in a conversational tone, addressing Hecate directly and expressing your intentions and desires. Share your gratitude for her presence and acknowledge her power and wisdom. Use descriptive language to paint a vivid picture of the qualities you seek to embody or the guidance you seek from Hecate. Feel free to include personal anecdotes or experiences that highlight your connection with her.

Personalisation and Adaptation:

Invocations should be personalised and adapted to suit your unique spiritual practices and intentions. Feel free to modify existing invocations or create your own from scratch. Incorporate elements that hold personal significance, such as specific symbols, deities, or experiences that resonate with Hecate's energy. Remember that invocations are an expression of your personal relationship with Hecate, and there is no one-size-fits-all approach. Trust your intuition and let it guide you in crafting invocations that are authentic to your own spiritual journey.

Ritual Structure:

Consider the structure of your rituals when incorporating invocations. You may choose to begin with a grounding meditation or a ritual cleansing to prepare yourself for the invocation. Place the invocation within the context of your ritual, whether it's lighting candles, making offerings, or performing other symbolic acts. Allow the invocation to serve as a focal point for your intentions and a channel for connecting with Hecate's energy.

Crafting invocations specific to Hecate is a personal and creative process. It allows practitioners to express their intentions, seek guidance, and honour Hecate's presence in a deeply meaningful way. Whether through poetry or prose, the invocations should reflect your unique connection with Hecate and convey the sincerity of your intentions. Remember to infuse your invocations with your own voice, emotions, and personal experiences to create a powerful and authentic connection with Hecate.

Offerings and Devotion:

Offerings are a meaningful way to express devotion, gratitude, and respect when invoking Hecate. They serve as tangible gestures of appreciation and establish a reciprocal relationship with the goddess. This section explores suitable offerings that can be presented to Hecate and highlights the significance of devotion and establishing a genuine connection through regular practices and acts of gratitude.

Candles:

Candles hold a significant role in Hecate's invocations. They symbolise illumination, transformation, and the guiding light that Hecate provides. Consider using black or purple candles to represent Hecate's association with the night and magic. Light the candles during your invocations to create a sacred ambiance and invoke Hecate's presence.

Incense:

Incense is another offering commonly used in Hecate's invocations. Choose scents that resonate with her energy, such as myrrh, patchouli, lavender, or frankincense. The fragrant smoke serves as a vehicle to carry your intentions and offerings to the realm of the divine, inviting Hecate's presence into the sacred space.

Herbs and Botanicals:

Offering herbs and botanicals associated with Hecate adds a natural and earthy dimension to your invocations. Mug wort, lavender, mandrake, yarrow, or rue are herbs often linked to Hecate's energy and magical properties. Place these herbs on your altar or burn them as an offering, infusing the space with their symbolic and aromatic qualities.

Crystals:

Crystals hold energetic vibrations that can enhance your connection with Hecate. Black obsidian, amethyst, moonstone, or labradorite are crystals associated with Hecate's energy. You can place them on your altar, hold them during invocations, or charge them under the moonlight as offerings to amplify your connection and intentions.

Symbolic Representations:

Incorporating symbolic representations of Hecate's associations can be a powerful offering. Consider including moon-related items like silver or crescent moon pendants, moon-shaped bowls, or lunar-themed artwork. Keys, torches, snakes, or triple moon symbols are also significant representations of Hecate's energy and can be added to your sacred space or presented as offerings.

Devotion and Regular Practices:

Devotion is an integral part of working with Hecate. Establish regular practices to honour her and deepen your connection. This could include setting aside dedicated time for meditation, divination, or spell work that focuses on Hecate's energy. Engage in acts of gratitude by offering prayers, expressing thanks, or dedicating specific rituals to her.

Offerings and devotion are personal expressions of your relationship with Hecate. Trust your intuition when selecting offerings and adapt them based on your own spiritual practices and resources. The most important aspect is the sincerity and heartfelt intention behind your offerings and acts of devotion.

By incorporating appropriate offerings, you not only express your gratitude and respect but also create a deeper connection with Hecate's energy. Regular practices of devotion and acts of gratitude solidify the bond between you and the goddess, fostering a genuine and reciprocal relationship that can enrich your spiritual journey.

Working with Hecate's Energy:

This section delves into practical ways of working with Hecate's energy beyond invocations. It discusses rituals and spell work that align with Hecate's associations, such as divination, shadow work, dreamwork, and intuitive development. It also explores how practitioners can seek Hecate's guidance and support in their personal and spiritual journeys.

Community Practices and Celebrations:

Hecate's influence extends beyond individual practices, and this section explores group rituals and celebrations dedicated to Hecate within pagan communities. It discusses communal invocations, guided meditations, and the significance of honouring Hecate during specific lunar phases or on significant dates in the pagan calendar.

Community Practices and Celebrations:

Hecate's influence transcends individual practices and extends into the realm of communal rituals and celebrations. This section delves into the collective worship of Hecate within pagan communities, exploring group invocations, guided meditations, and the significance of honouring Hecate during specific lunar phases or on significant dates in the pagan calendar.

Group Invocations:

Group invocations of Hecate create a powerful collective energy that enhances the connection with the goddess. During group rituals, participants can take turns reciting invocations, sharing their intentions, and collectively calling upon Hecate's guidance and presence. The shared experience amplifies the energy and fosters a sense of unity among the participants.

Guided Meditations:

Guided meditations can be used in group settings to connect with Hecate's energy and explore her realms. A facilitator guides the participants through a meditation journey that invokes the imagery of crossroads, the moonlit night, or the realms of the underworld, allowing everyone to experience a deeper connection with Hecate's energies. This shared experience can be transformative and enhance the sense of community.

Lunar Celebrations:

Hecate's association with lunar phases makes lunar celebrations a fitting way to honour her. Gatherings can be organised during the new moon, full moon, or other significant lunar phases to honour Hecate's transformative powers and her connection to the cycles of life and death. These celebrations can include rituals, invocations, offerings, and communal activities that align with Hecate's energy and intentions.

Seasonal Festivals:

Pagan communities often celebrate seasonal festivals that correspond to the cycles of nature. Some festivals, such as Samhain, Beltane, or the Winter Solstice, hold significance in relation to Hecate's attributes and the liminal spaces she represents. During these festivals, the community can come together to honour Hecate's role as a guide, protector, and guardian of thresholds, and engage in rituals and ceremonies that invoke her presence.

Crossroad Gatherings:

As Hecate is the goddess of crossroads, organising gatherings at literal crossroads can be a unique way to honour her. These gatherings can include communal rituals, invocations, and offerings that acknowledge Hecate's presence as the guardian of crossroads and seek her guidance in navigating life's choices and transitions. It's essential to ensure the safety and legality of gathering at crossroads and to respect the environment in which the rituals take place.

Pagan Calendar Celebrations:

Within the pagan calendar, there are specific dates and festivals that hold particular significance in relation to Hecate's mythology and attributes. These celebrations provide opportunities for individuals and communities to honour Hecate, deepen their connection with her energy, and participate in rituals dedicated to her. Here are two notable celebrations associated with Hecate:

Hecate's Deipnon:

Hecate's Deipnon is a ritual observance traditionally held on the last day of the lunar month, usually the night before the new moon. Deipnon, meaning "dinner" or "supper" in Greek, refers to the ritual meal offered to Hecate. This celebration involves purifying and cleansing the home, preparing offerings, and placing them at a crossroads or an outdoor altar.

During Hecate's Deipnon, participants may clean their homes, sweep away negative energy, and offer food, wine, herbs, or other symbolic items to Hecate. This ritual act is believed to appease and honour her, seeking her protection and guidance. It is also a time for personal reflection, releasing what no longer serves, and preparing for new beginnings with the upcoming new moon.

Rite of Her Sacred Fires:

The Rite of Her Sacred Fires is a global or local observance dedicated to Hecate held on May 16th, inspired by the work of Sorita d'Este, a writer and priestess dedicated to Hecate. This celebration aims to bring together practitioners from different paths and traditions to honour Hecate in unison.

During the Rite of Her Sacred Fires, individuals and groups perform their own rituals and invocations, creating a collective energy of devotion and reverence for Hecate. Participants light candles or bonfires, offer prayers, and engage in personal or group activities that symbolise their connection with Hecate's energy and her diverse aspects. This celebration serves as a powerful opportunity to connect with a global community of Hecate devotees and experience the strength of collective devotion.

These are just a couple of examples of pagan calendar celebrations that provide dedicated occasions to honour and invoke Hecate. It's important to note that practices and dates may vary among different pagan traditions and individual practitioners. Exploring local pagan communities, online forums, and resources dedicated to Hecate can provide further insights into specific dates and celebrations relevant to her worship.

Participating in these pagan calendar celebrations dedicated to Hecate allows individuals to connect with her energy on a deeper level, align themselves with the rhythms of nature, and join a wider community of devotees who share a similar reverence for this powerful goddess.

Community practices and celebrations dedicated to Hecate foster a sense of shared devotion and connection among pagan communities. By coming together, practitioners can amplify the energy of their individual practices and create a collective experience that honours Hecate's guidance, wisdom, and transformative powers. These group rituals and celebrations deepen the understanding and reverence for Hecate, creating a supportive and empowering community of like-minded individuals on their spiritual journeys.

Conclusion.

In conclusion, the journey through the mythological realm of Hecate, the powerful goddess of crossroads, magic, and the moon, has been a profound exploration of her multifaceted nature and significant role in ancient Greek mythology and worship. Throughout this book, we have delved into the depths of Hecate's legends, symbols, and associations, uncovering the rich tapestry of her divine presence.

Hecate, with her triple form and ever-watchful eyes, embodies the essence of liminality and transition. She presides over crossroads, those sacred meeting points between realms, and guides travellers along their paths. Her presence at these intersections signifies not only physical choices but also metaphorical decisions, marking pivotal moments in life's journey.

As the goddess of magic and witchcraft, Hecate holds a special place in the hearts of practitioners and covens today. Her association with the underworld and necromancy links her to the mysteries of life and death, as well as the realms beyond. She is revered as a guardian of secrets, a bestower of wisdom, and a guide for those who seek to navigate the realms of the unseen.

Hecate's connection to the moon and its phases adds another layer of depth to her symbolism. She embodies the waxing and waning cycles, the ebb and flow of life's rhythms. From the youthful maiden to the nurturing mother and the wise crone, Hecate encompasses the full spectrum of feminine power and wisdom.

Throughout history, individuals and households have paid homage to Hecate through personal devotion, setting up altars and shrines dedicated to her. Public festivals and ceremonies held at crossroads and sacred sites have honoured her presence and sought her blessings. The keys, torches, serpents, and dogs associated with her have become iconic symbols, representing her domain and influence.

The syncretism and Hellenistic influences on Hecate have further expanded her reach, weaving her into the tapestry of various cultures and belief systems. Her role as a patroness of witchcraft, the guide of souls, and the protector of boundaries has resonated across time and across civilizations.

In the modern world, Hecate continues to inspire and empower. Her wisdom, strength, and magical prowess are embraced by those who seek her guidance and blessings. Through rituals, spells, and invocations, practitioners invoke her energy and tap into the transformative power she embodies.

As we conclude this book, let us carry with us the ancient wisdom of Hecate, the goddess of crossroads. May her lessons in liminality, magic, and lunar cycles remind us to embrace change, make choices with intention, and honour the interconnectedness of all things. In the crossroads of our lives, may we find the guidance and protection that Hecate, the torchbearer, offers us on our individual and collective journeys.

Appendixes.

The Full Moon Invocation of Hecate's Power: -

Ingredients:
- A white candle
- A small bowl of water
- A piece of paper and pen
- A sacred space where you can perform the ritual undisturbed

Instructions:

. Set up your sacred space, ensuring it is clean and free from distractions. Place the white candle in the centre, surrounded by the bowl of water.

Light the white candle, representing the illuminating power of the Full Moon.

Take a moment to ground yourself and connect with the energy of the Full Moon. Close your eyes, breathe deeply, and envision the moon's radiant light surrounding you.

Hold the piece of paper and pen in your hands and meditate on your intentions. Reflect on what you wish to manifest, what abundance you seek, or any specific guidance you desire from Hecate.

When you feel ready, write your intentions or requests on the paper. Be clear and concise, focusing on your true desires.

Fold the paper and place it in the bowl of water, symbolising the act of releasing your intentions to Hecate and the moon's energy.

Speak the following invocation, or feel free to create your own heartfelt words:

"Divine Hecate, Goddess of the Crossroads,
I stand before you on this night of power.
As the Full Moon shines brightly in the sky,
I call upon your abundant and illuminating energy.
Hecate, hear my voice, guide my way.

> Grant me the strength to manifest my desires,
> The wisdom to see my path clearly,
> And the courage to embrace transformation.
> With the moon's fullness as my witness,
> I release my intentions and dreams to your care.
> May your guidance and blessings empower me,
> And may my actions align with divine will.
> Hecate, I thank you for your presence,
> For your wisdom and transformative power.
> As the Full Moon shines upon me,
> May your light illuminate my path ahead.
> So be it."

Allow the candle to burn down safely or extinguish it with gratitude, knowing that your intentions have been sent forth to Hecate and the Full Moon's energy.

Leave the folded paper in the bowl of water overnight, allowing the energy to infuse and work its magic. In the morning, dispose of the paper by burying it in the earth or releasing it to a flowing body of water.

Remember, as you perform this spell, do so with respect and a genuine connection to Hecate's energy. May the Full Moon's abundant and illuminating power bring forth the manifestation of your true desires. Blessed be.

It's essential to practice responsible and ethical magic. Avoid casting spells that interfere with the free will of others or cause harm. Always use your intentions for the highest good of all.

Full Moon Invocation of Hecate's Wisdom and Guidance:

Ingredients:
- A black candle
- A silver or white cloth
- A small bowl of water
- A key or symbolic representation of a key
- A piece of obsidian or moonstone
- A bell or chime
- A journal and pen
- Optional: Hecate's sigil or image

Instructions:

Set up your sacred space, preferably outdoors where you can see the Full Moon, or in a quiet, well-ventilated area indoors. Lay the silver or white cloth on a table or altar.

Place the black candle in the centre of the cloth, surrounded by the small bowl of water. If you have Hecate's sigil or image, you can place it nearby as well.

Light the black candle, representing the transformative and mysterious energy of Hecate. Take a moment to breathe and centre yourself.

Hold the key or symbolic representation of a key in your hands. Close your eyes and imagine Hecate's presence surrounding you. Feel her wisdom and guidance flowing into the key, symbolising the unlocking of hidden knowledge.

With the key in hand, speak the following invocation, or feel free to use your own words:

"Great Hecate, Goddess of the Crossroads,
I stand before you on this sacred night,
Under the watchful gaze of the Full Moon's light.

Goddess of wisdom, magic, and mystery,
I call upon your presence, I call upon thee.
Open the gates to hidden realms and truths,
Guide me on a journey to wisdom's roots.
Hecate, I seek your guidance and insight,
As the Full Moon shines with radiant might.
Unlock the mysteries that lie within,
Grant me the knowledge to begin again.
With this key, I embrace your power,
May your wisdom guide me every hour.
Blessed Hecate, hear my call,
As the moon rises, I surrender all."

Place the key or symbolic representation on the altar, near the candle. Take the obsidian or moonstone in your hands, feeling its grounding and protective energy. Reflect on any questions or guidance you seek from Hecate.

When ready, ring the bell or chime three times to signal your intention to connect with Hecate's energy and open yourself to her guidance.

Sit in meditation for a few moments, embracing the stillness and allowing any insights or messages to come through. You may choose to journal your experiences afterward.

Offer gratitude to Hecate for her presence and guidance. Express your thanks for her wisdom and transformative power. Blow out the candle, symbolising the end of the ritual.

As you perform this ritual, do so with reverence and respect for Hecate's energy. Be open to receiving her guidance and insights. May the Full Moon illuminate your path and bring forth the wisdom you seek. Blessed be.

Adapt the ritual according to your personal beliefs and preferences. It's important to practice responsible and ethical rituals, always seeking the highest good for yourself and others.

Evoking Hecate's Blessings in the Waxing Moon:

Ingredients:
- A silver or white candle
- A black cloth or altar cloth
- A small bowl of salt or herbs (such as lavender or sage)
- A key or symbolic representation of a key
- A piece of amethyst or clear quartz
- A journal and pen
- Optional: Hecate's sigil or image

Instructions:

Prepare your sacred space by placing the black cloth or altar cloth on a table or altar. Arrange the silver or white candle in the centre, along with the small bowl of salt or herbs.

Light the silver or white candle, symbolising the illumination and growth of the waxing moon. Take a moment to ground yourself and connect with the energy of the moon.

Hold the key or symbolic representation of a key in your hands, visualising the blessings and wisdom of Hecate flowing into it. Set the key on the altar or hold it throughout the ritual if you prefer.

Sprinkle a pinch of salt or herbs into the bowl, representing purification and protection. As you do so, say:

"By the power of the waxing moon's light,
I purify this space, making it sacred and bright.
Hecate, I invite you to join me here,
In this moment of magic, love, and cheer."

If you have Hecate's sigil or image, place it on the altar or hold it in your hands. Alternatively, you can visualise her presence in your mind's eye.

Hold the amethyst or clear quartz in your hands, feeling its soothing and clarifying energy. Set your intentions for the waxing moon phase, focusing on growth, abundance, and positive transformation. Speak your intentions aloud, or silently in your mind.

Take a few moments to reflect on the blessings you wish to invite into your life. Write them down in your journal, capturing your desires, dreams, and goals. You can also write a letter to Hecate, expressing your intentions and seeking her guidance.

Sit in meditation, visualising the waxing moon's energy surrounding you. Imagine Hecate's presence beside you, offering her guidance and support. Feel the energy of growth and transformation permeate your being.

When you are ready, express your gratitude to Hecate for her presence and blessings. Blow out the candle, symbolising the end of the ritual.

Adapt this ritual to align with your personal beliefs and preferences. Open yourself to the energies of the waxing moon and Hecate's guidance. May your intentions manifest and your journey be blessed. Blessed be.

Practice this ritual responsibly and ethically, always seeking the highest good for yourself and others.

Embracing Release and Transformation with Hecate in the Waning Moon:

Ingredients:
- A black candle
- A black cloth or altar cloth
- A small bowl of water
- Dried herbs or incense (such as myrrh or frankincense)
- A piece of obsidian or black tourmaline
- A journal and pen
- Optional: Hecate's sigil or image

Instructions:

Set up your sacred space by placing the black cloth or altar cloth on a table or altar. Arrange the black candle in the centre, along with the small bowl of water.

Light the black candle, symbolising the release and transformation that comes with the waning moon phase. Take a moment to ground yourself and connect with the energy of the moon.

Hold the piece of obsidian or black tourmaline in your hands, feeling its grounding and protective energy. Set it on the altar or keep it with you throughout the ritual.

Sprinkle a few drops of water into the bowl, representing purification and emotional release. As you do so, say:

"Hecate, goddess of the waning moon,
Guide me in my journey of release and tune.
With this water, I cleanse and let go,
Allowing transformation and healing to flow."

If you have Hecate's sigil or image, place it on the altar or hold it in your hands. Alternatively, you can visualise her presence in your mind's eye.

Light the dried herbs or incense, allowing the smoke to fill the air. Take a moment to inhale the scent, focusing on releasing any negative or stagnant energies from your life. Visualise them dissipating into the smoke.

Reflect on the aspects of your life or yourself that you wish to release and transform. Write them down in your journal, acknowledging the patterns, emotions, or situations that no longer serve you. Express your willingness to let go and invite positive change.

Sit in meditation, focusing on your breath and allowing yourself to fully embrace the energy of release and transformation. Visualise Hecate's presence, offering her guidance and support as you navigate this process.

When you are ready, express your gratitude to Hecate for her presence and assistance. Blow out the candle, symbolising the completion of the ritual.

Adapt this ritual to suit your beliefs and preferences. Open yourself to the energies of the waning moon and Hecate's transformative power. May you find liberation and embrace positive change. Blessed be.

Practice this ritual responsibly and ethically, always seeking the highest good for yourself and others.

About the Author

As a lover of dogs and an ardent seeker of adventure, I possesses an insatiable curiosity that extends beyond the ordinary. With an unwavering passion for the mystical realms of the Craft, Paganism, and Wicca, I have delved deep into the secrets and wonders of these ancient traditions. Through many years of dedicated practice, I have honed my expertise in the art of invoking the goddess, harnessing the elemental forces, and aligning their magic with the captivating power of the moon. Fuelled by a profound connection to the lunar cycles, I have developed a unique understanding of how to infuse rituals, spells, and magic with the moon's potent energy. In my journey of spiritual exploration, I have discovered that the moon holds an unparalleled allure, serving as a guide, a source of inspiration, and a transformative force. My intimate knowledge of invoking the moon's influence has become a cornerstone of my craft, enabling me to create deeply profound and effective magical experiences. Through my writing, I seek to empower others to embrace the enchantment of Paganism, Wicca, and the Craft while tapping into the profound wisdom and energy of the moon. Step into the world of magic, and embark on a journey that will deepen your connection to the mystical forces that surround us, elevate your magical practice, and ignite the wild, daring spirit within

9 798822 352839